ReqIF Studio

Requirements Engineering Platform

based on Eclipse

Michael Jastram (Editor)

Contents

1. Introduction

The importance of requirements has been recognized for a long time. And with the advent of computer-aided engineering tools, a number of proprietary solutions have popped up all over the place. While this has helped organizations to manage their requirements more efficiently, interoperability became a major issue.

The development of the ReqIF standard for requirements exchange finally provided a standard, feature-rich way of accessing requirements data. Eclipse was the obvious choice for a reference implementation of this open standard. The result is the Eclipse Requirements Modeling Framework, a complete, open source, user-friendly implementation of ReqIF.

This handbook is a comprehensive documentation of the ReqIF Studio tool, which is based on Eclipse RMF. All answers with respect to tool use should be answered here. Furthermore, it contains a small tutorial (Chapter 3) to get you started quickly.

Keep in mind that tools are meant to support processes, not the other way around. ReqIF Studio is a flexible tool, and it can be tailored to support your processes. But development processes are explicitly outside the scope of this handbook.

1.1   ReqIF.academy

For a tool to be useful, it is crucial to have quick access to all related information. Reqif.academy[1] has been created for exactly that purpose. Instead of hunting information down from all over the web, ReqIF.academy provides all information in one spot.

> ▶ **ReqIF.academy.** ReqIF.academy (https://reqif.academy) is an online knowledge base for ReqIF and ReqIF Studio. Visit it for videos, templates, checklists, references and of course software and this handbook.

At ReqIF.academy, you find the following content:

Workshops. There will be regular physical workshops regarding ReqIF. The current schedule is prominently posted.

Videos. Videos cover ReqIF Studio, requirements exchange, the Requirements Interchange Format, and much more. New videos are added on a regular basis.

Software. Software includes ReqIF Studio itself, for various platforms, and a number of free and premium software components.

Books. A number of free and premium eBooks, including this handbook as PDF or in print.

References. Many cheat sheets and other references, including one for the ReqIF standard.

FAQs. A number of continuously updated Frequently Asked Questions (FAQs).

Checklists. For commonly performed tasks, you can download appropriate checklists.

Templates. We will continuously add templates to the library, to help you get started quickly.

Papers. The library includes various publications related to the subject matter.

1.2   ReqIF Studio, RMF and ProR

There are a few derivatives of the RMF project that may be confusing. The following will help you to understand the ecosystem and how the pieces fit together:

RMF. The Requirements Modeling Framework (RMF) is an open

---

[1]https://reqif.academy

source project that is managed by the Eclipse Foundation. It consists of software code, documentation, mailing lists, online forum, etc. It is a software framework, and you need an application to use it. Like:

ReqIF Studio. This is an application that is based on RMF and maintained by the company Formal Mind. For users who "just want to edit requirements", this is the most convenient way of getting started. ReqIF Studio contains some useful extensions to RMF, which are called:

Essentials. The company Formal Mind created this collection of add-ons that make RMF much more usable. For instance, Essentials allows for the editing and rendering of formatted text.

ProR. ProR is the old name of the user interface that allows users to work with ReqIF-based requirements. You can build ProR from the RMF sources, but there is no ready-to-use download of ProR.

1.3   System Requirements

ReqIF Studio and RMF require at least Java 6 and Eclipse 3.8. Some features of ProR Essentials require Java 7 from Oracle (not openJDK). Of course, you can use newer versions of Java without problems.

ReqIF Studio is based on Eclipse Luna (4.4). This has not been upgraded, as some large organizations still use fairly old versions of Java. Using a newer version of Eclipse would require a newer version of Java as well.

1.4   Conventions

Throughout this book you'll see the following conventions:

(i) Tips are marked with this icon. They usually summarize how to work more effectively. Details about the subject matter are found in the text.

(!) Warnings are marked with this icon. They point out things that can go wrong, or important steps that are easily missed.

■ **Example 1.1** Examples often demonstrate how a concept is applied in practice. They will be marked with a black square at the beginning and at the end, as shown with this text.　■

When referring to MENUS or USER INTERFACE ELEMENTS, they are shown like here on gray background in small capitals.

When we introduce a new *term* or want it to stand out, it will be marked like *this* in the text. Often this is done only the first time that it appears.

Terms that represent ReqIF model elements (e.g. SpecObject) are capitalized. Sometimes, we abbreviate them, for instance "SpecElement" instead of the full "SpecElementWithAttributes". They will still be capitalized to indicate that these are model elements.

▶ **Definition.** Definitions appear throughout the text and concisely define new terms. They appear in the text wherever they are introduced first. Please take advantage of the index at the end of the book to quickly find definitions.

1.5 Acknowledgements

Many parties were involved in the creation of RMF. We would like to thank the core team that made it possible.

The roots of this project were created by Andreas Graf, Michael Jastram and Nirmal Sasidharan, who joined together individual projects to create RMF. Their efforts were financed by the research projects itea Verde and FP7 Deploy. RMF was assembled at the Eclipse Foundation, where it has been active ever since. Figure 1.1 shows four of the five RMF Committers at a joint coding session (missing is Andreas Graf).

We would also like to thank Mathias Legrand for providing The Legrand Orange Book template[2].

1.6 License

This work, or parts thereof, are licensed under the Eclipse Public License Version 1.0[3] as part of the Eclipse Requirements Modeling Framework (RMF) project at eclipse.org/rmf[4].

---

[2]http://www.latextemplates.com/template/the-legrand-orange-book
[3]https://www.eclipse.org/legal/epl-v10.html
[4]https://www.eclipse.org/rmf

Figure 1.1: The RMF team during a Sprint in April 2012 in Düsseldorf, Germany: Lukas Ladenberger, Mark Brörkens, Ingo Weigelt, Said Salem and Michael Jastram (left to right)

Some parts of this document are licensed as Apache 2.0 License[5] and are aggregated into this handbook. The sources are part of the Teaching System Engineering Project.

The remainder of this document is copyrighted by Formal Mind GmbH. All rights reserved.

(i)   If you want to support open source software, consider supporting the project by becoming a member of the ReqIF Academy[6]. The ReqIF Academy is a library of ReqIF knowledge with mostly free content. A premium membership will provide you with additional content and support this software.

1.7 Further Reading

There are a number of useful resources, both for beginners and advanced users.

---

[5]http://www.apache.org/licenses/LICENSE-2.0.html
[6]https://reqif.academy

1.7.1 Online Resources

There are many useful resources on the internet:

ReqIF Academy.

This online library provides lots of free ReqIF-related content, like videos, checklists and more. There is also additional premium content. https://reqif.academy.

Formal Mind Blog and Newsletter.

The blog provides you with useful information regarding updates, new features, events, etc. roughly once a month. It is also published as a newsletter. Sign up at http://formalmind.com/newsletter.

Systems Engineering Trends (German)

This weekly blog covers many Systems Engineering-related topics, including requirements engineering and open source. Sign up at http://se-trends.de.

Eclipse Requirements Modeling Framework.

ReqIF Studio is based on the Eclipse Requirements Modeling Framework. Visit eclipse.org/rmf[7] for information and news on this open source project.

1.7.2 Requirements

ReqIF Studio assumes some basic knowledge regarding requirements management. Here are some pointers:

Mark Book.

This book (Managing Requirements Knowledge) strives to collect the state of the art on requirements engineering knowledge. It includes a chapter on ProR, RMF and ReqIF, which is available for free [Jastram, 2013].

1.7.3 Requirements Interchange Format

ReqIF Studio is based on the Requirements Interchange Format. These resources may be useful:

---

[7]http://eclipse.org/rmf

ReqIF Academy.
This online library contains lots of content and is updated regularly
[Formal Mind, 2016].

Open Up.
This article, published in RE Magazine, provides a good overview
of the Requirements Interchange Format (ReqIF) [Jastram, 2014].

1.8 License Manager

ReqIF Studio allows the installation of commercial components
that require licenses. Licenses can be acquired through a premium
membership of ReqIF Academy[8]. You will receive a file ending in
.license.

> ⓘ Once installed, licenses are available for the user account.
> In other words, even for multiple ReqIF Studio installa-
> tions and workspaces, the license has to be installed only
> once.

1.8.1 License Manager Dialog

The license manager shows an arbitrary number of licenses, one
per row. For each license, the following pieces of information are
shown in columns, as shown in Figure 1.2.

Component. The commercial component that the license is for.

Licensed to. The email of the person the component is licensed
to. All licenses must be licensed to the same email. If you
purchased multiple components with different emails, please
contact Formal Mind.

Expiration. The expiration date of the license.

Installed. Whether the component is installed or not. If it is
not, you can install it by selecting the license and pressing
INSTALL COMPONENT....

The License Manager has the following buttons:

Add License... Adds a license, which is a file ending in .license.
It will be added to the list of installed licenses.

Buy or Renew License... Automatic renewal is currently not
supported. Please visit the Formal Mind Web Store to
purchase a new license.

---

[8]https://reqif.academy

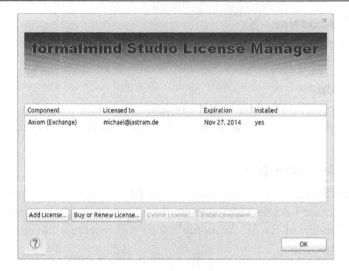

Figure 1.2: The license manager with one license installed

Delete License... This removes the selected license. This is useful for expired licenses, for instance.

Install Component... If the licensed component is not yet installed, you can initiate the installationby selecting the license and pressing INSTALL COMPONENT.... This is described in Section 1.8.2.

> (i) Multiple Licenses for the same component can be installed at the same time. You can press DELETE LICENSE... to remove unused licenses.

1.8.2 Installing Components

Once a license is installed, the component itself needs to be installed (if it has not yet been installed already). This is done by clicking on INSTALL COMPONENT..., which launches the Eclipse Marketplace for Formal Mind components, as shown in Figure 1.3.

Browse to the component that you would like to install. Click on INSTALL and follow the installation instructions.

Figure 1.3: Installation of a component via the Formal Mind Marketplace

2. Overview

This chapter provides a high-level overview of requirements engineering, requirements tooling, ReqIF and the terminology.

2.1 Requirements Engineering & Management

This book is concerned with ReqIF Studio a tool for requirements engineering.

▶ **Requirements Engineering.** "Requirements engineering (RE) refers to the process of formulating, documenting and maintaining software requirements." (Wikipedia[a]).

Requirements are typically recorded in unstructured natural language. However, it is possible to use a formal language as well. Of high interest these days is model-driven requirements engineering.

[a]http://en.wikipedia.org/wiki/Requirements_engineering

But engineering the requirements is not enough: they need to be *managed*.

▶ **Requirements Management.** "Requirements management is the process of documenting, analyzing, tracing, prioritizing and agreeing on requirements and then controlling change and communicating to relevant stakeholders. It is a continuous process throughout a project." (Wikipedia[a]).

---
[a]http://en.wikipedia.org/wiki/Requirements_management

2.2 Tools

There are many tools available for requirements engineering. These include free or cheap ones, like Microsoft Word and Excel, Wikis and issue trackers. There are expensive, professional ones available, like IBM® Rational® DOORS®, PTC Integrity or Visure IRQA. Lately, there are also web-based tools, like Siemens Polarion.

ReqIF Studio falls into the category of free tools. But compared to the ones mentioned, it contains important features from professional tools, including traceability and typed attributes. Further, by taking advantage of the Eclipse ecosystem, the tool can be augmented by plug-ins for version support, model integration and much more.

(i) Professional support, commercial components and integration services are available from Formal Mind[1], via a ReqIF Academy premium membership[2].

2.3 Requirements Interchange Format (ReqIF)

ReqIF stands for Requirements Interchange Format. It is an exchange format for requirements and a data model. ReqIF Studio is an editor that can directly view and modify ReqIF data.

ReqIF was created to support the exchange of requirements across organizations. For instance, it allows a manufacturer to send requirements to suppliers. The suppliers can then comment and review the requirements, or they can create a system specification that is linked to the requirements.

ReqIF is an official OMG standard[3].

---
[1]http://formalmind.com
[2]https://reqif.academy
[3]http://www.omg.org/spec/ReqIF/

ReqIF uses its own terminology. Section 2.4 defines the ReqIF vocabulary and how it relates to the terms used in classical requirements engineering.

2.3.1 ReqIF History

For technical and organizational reasons, two companies in the manufacturing industry are rarely able to work on the same requirements repository and sometimes do not work with the same requirements authoring tools. A generic, non-proprietary format for requirements information is required to cross the chasm and to satisfy the urgent industry need for exchanging requirement information between different companies without losing the advantage of requirements management at the organizations' borders.

The Requirements Interchange Format (ReqIF) described in this RFC defines such a tool-independent exchange format. Requirement information is exchanged by transferring XML documents that comply to the ReqIF format.

In 2004, the HIS (Hersteller Initiative Software), a panel of Germany's automotive manufacturers (Daimler, VW, Porsche, Audi and BMW Group) developed the idea of creating the "Requirements Interchange Format". In 2005, the first version of that format was presented at the REConf, a conference about requirements engineering and management, in Munich. In 2008, the HIS Steering Committee decided that the internationalization and maintenance of the Requirements Interchange Format should be proceeded with the ProSTEP iViP Association. A project was set up and a team was built that includes members of the ProSTEP iViP Association, representatives of manufacturing companies (Audi, BMW Group, Daimler, VW, Bosch and Continental), tool vendors (Atego, IBM, MKS) and development partners (HOOD GmbH, PROSTEP AG).

Further reading: The HIS Exchange Process for Requirements–all you ever wanted to know[4] at ReqIF.academy.

The ReqIF team expects that making the Requirements Interchange Format an OMG standard increases the number of

---

[4]https://reqif.academy/faq/his-process/

interoperable exchange tool implementations on the market, fosters the trust of companies exchanging requirement information in the exchange format and provides safety of investments to tool vendors.

2.3.2 Previous Versions of ReqIF

This document is submitted as RFC of the Requirements Interchange Format (ReqIF) to the OMG. Before the submission, the Requirements Interchange Format has been a specification proposed by the HIS and in its latest version, a recommendation of ProSTEP iViP. For these versions, the abbreviation "RIF" has been applied. The HIS released the Requirements Interchange Format as RIF 1.0, RIF 1.0a, RIF 1.1; RIF 1.1a and the ProSTEP iViP released the recommendation RIF 1.2.

As the acronym RIF has an ambiguous meaning within the OMG, the acronym ReqIF has been introduced to separate it from the W3C's Rule Interchange Format. ReqIF 1.0 is the direct successor of the ProSTEP iViP recommendation RIF 1.2.

> The ReqIF Studio user interface does not currently support RIF.

2.3.3 Internal Attributes

ReqIF allows users to define the attributes that SpecObjects may carry. In addition to these, there are a number of internal attributes that are defined by the ReqIF standard. Examples include an internal ID or the last change timestamp.

These internal attributes are rarely of interest to users who just want to work with requirements. However, they may be of interest to tool experts, or may be inspected for troubleshooting.

Internal attributes can be accessed from the Properties View, using the ALL ATTRIBUTES tab.

2.4 Terminology

Working with ReqIF Studio can be confusing as it uses the terminology from ReqIF. For instance, ReqIF uses *SpecObjects*, rather than *requirements*. In the following, we define the more important terms. More are defined throughout the document. You can use the index to find the definition of terms.

(i) This book uses ReqIF terminology throughout. Please refer to this chapter to understand the meaning of these terms.

A *ReqIF model* is the data structure that holds all the information together. In practical terms, it's just a file, that usually ends in .REQIF or .REQIFZ. It contains not just the requirements, but also the data types of those requirements and a lot of other stuff. It has been described in detail in Section 2.3.

▶ **ReqIF.** ReqIF is an XML-based format for requirements, intended to be used as an exchange format. It is an open OMG standard and described in detail in Section 2.3. The XML data is typically stored in a with with the extension .REQIF. It is also possible to store the ReqIF file together with associated data (embedded objects) or other ReqIF files. These are then stored in a ZIP archive with the extension .REQIFZ.

Before defining the most important elements, we will provide a brief overview with a concrete example.

2.4.1 The Most Important ReqIF Elements

Figure 2.1 shows a simple ReqIF model, open in ReqIF Studio.

The SPECIFICATION EDITOR (the central table) shows the first four *SpecObjects*, as visualized in a specification. The tree-like structure is recognizable: INF-1 is a node with three children, REQ-1, REQ-2 and REQ-3 (this can be seen by the indentation). Let's look at INF-1 and REQ-1. When one is selected in the main pain, it's attributes appear in the PROPERTIES VIEW, the pane at the bottom.

INF-1 has two *Attributes*, "Description" and "ID". The *SpecType* is "Information Type" (shown as the header in the PROPERTIES VIEW).

REQ-1, REQ-2, and REQ-3 have three Attributes, "Description", "ID" and "Status" (this is not obvious from the figure). To accommodate this, a column called "Status" has been created. As the "Information Type" has no "Status" attribute, it is not shown in the PROPERTIES VIEW.

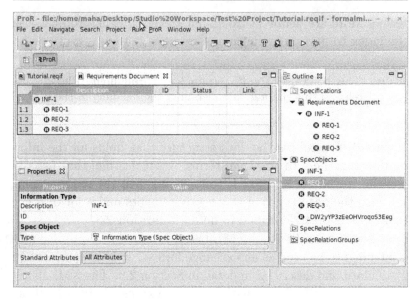

Figure 2.1: Specification example

2.4.2 SpecElements

A requirement is called a *SpecObject*. This is arguably the most important element in ReqIF, the actual requirements that you are working with. The SpecObjects of a ReqIF model can be directly accessed in ReqIF Studio via the outline. It is more common to access them via a *Specification*. When a SpecObject is selected, its details (attributes and internal information) are shown in the PROPERTIES VIEW.

▶ **SpecObject.** A SpecObject is a data structure for storing requirements information. It has a number of *attributes*. The most typical attributes include the requirements text and a human-readable ID. A *SpecType* determines the attributes of the SpecObject. It is a *SpecElement*.

There are other elements in ReqIF that have a type and attributes. We call these *SpecElements*, although in the official ReqIF specification, they are called *SpecElementsWithAttributes*.

▶ **SpecElement.** A SpecElement is an abstract ReqIF element that has a *SpecType* and *Attributes*. Concrete manifestations include *SpecObjects*, *Specifications*, *SpecRelations* and *SpecRelationGroups*.

Creating links between SpecObjects is a central functionality of requirements tools. In ReqIF terminology, links are called *SpecRelations*.

▶ **SpecRelation.** A SpecRelation is a data structure for connecting two SpecObjects. It contains a *source* and a *target* reference to the SpecObjects that are connected. As a SpecRelation is a SpecElement, it has a type and attributes.

SpecObjects do not have any particular order. SpecObjects can be organized into a tree-like structure by using a *Specification*. A Specification is a root element for a tree of SpecObjects. The SpecObjects are referenced. This means that the same SpecObject can be referenced multiple times, both within one Specification or in different Specifications.

▶ **Specification.** A Specification is a data structure for organizing SpecObjects into a tree structure. This tree consists of references. As a Specification is a SpecElement, it has a type and attributes.

All SpecElements have a *SpecType*. A SpecType defines *AttributeDefinitions*, which defines the attributes for the SpecElement of that type.

■ **Example 2.1** An AttributeDefinition is just a data type with a label. Slightly simplified, examples would be:

- Attribute *ID* of type *String*
- Attribute *Status* of type *Enumeration* with the values *accepted* and *rejected*
- Attribute *ReqIF.Text* of type *XHTML* (rich text).

                                                                                    ■

▶ **SpecType.** The SpecType defines a set of *AttributeDefinitions*. A SpecElement with the given type has the attributes defined by the AttributeDefinitions.

▶ **AttributeDefinition.** An AttributeDefinition belongs to a SpecType. It consists of a label and a DatatypeDefinition, which provides the type. Some AttributeDefinitions can be configured further. AttributeDefinitions can also have a *default value*.

Lastly, there are seven *DatatypeDefinitions*, some of which can be customized further.

► **DatatypeDefinition.**   DatatypeDefinitions are the fundamental types in ReqIF and include:

- Boolean – true or false
- Integer – the range can be customized
- Real – range and precision can be customized
- Date – also includes the time
- String – the maximum length can be customized
- Enumeration – both single and multiple choice are sup-
  ported
- XHTML – allow embedding objects of any type

2.4.3 Comparing Excel and ReqIF

With the basic terminology in place, we have a quick look at
the ReqIF Studio user interface and compare it with Excel. We
do this, as most readers will be familiar with Excel, and it is
sometimes used for simple requirements engineering.

Specification. (Excel-equivalent: Sheet) A ReqIF model can
have an arbitrary number of Specifications. In the GUI, it
is represented as an Excel-like grid view (see Figure 2.1).

The *Specification* is the "container" for the requirements.
Think of an Excel document that allows you to create an
arbitrary number of sheets. Each sheet can be compared to
a single Specification. Most notable differences are: (1) the
Specifications are *references* rather than independent entities
(which means that the same requirement can be referenced
and can appear in multiple places); (2) A Specification
manages a hierarchy of requirements, while an Excel sheet
is a flat list. This is shown in the Figure, where INF-1 is
the parent to three requirements. The hierarchy is visible
both in the main editor, as well as in the outline.

SpecObject. (Excel-equivalent: Row) A SpecObject represents
the actual requirement, and is typically organized in a Specification.

Each row in the Excel spread sheet is the equivalent of a
SpecObject. A requirement typically has a number of attributes. Again compared to Excel, each row in a sheet
represents a requirement and each cell represents an attribute. However, in Excel, all rows have the same columns

(all requirements have the same attributes), while ReqIF allows mixing SpecObjects of different SpecTypes. Also, not all attributes need to be shown in a Specification.

Figure 2.1 shows in the OUTLINE VIEW a flat list of all SpecObjects. For instance, the SpecObject _DW2y... is not referenced in the Specification at all. Selecting a SpecObject shows its SpecType (in the figure, it is "Information Type") and all attributes (in the figure, "Description" and "ID").

Attribute. (Excel-equivalent: Cell) An attribute holds the actual content of a SpecObject.

In Excel, a new attribute is simply created by putting a column header on a column. In ReqIF, columns are created via STUDIO | COLUMN CONFIGURATION, or by clicking on ℝ. But content will only be shown if the SpecObject of that row has an attribute of that name.

Besides the actual text of the requirement, typical attributes include ID, status, etc. Note that there are no "standard" attributes. However, the ProSTEP Implementor Forum defined a recommendation for a set of standard attributes.

2.5 ReqIF Implementor Forum

We already mentioned the ProStep ReqIF Implementor Forum. ReqIF Studio is designed to be fully compliant with the implementor guide that got produced by the Forum.

2.5.1 Conversation ID

ReqIF Studio supports the management of an ID in the *ToolExtensions* that is used for tracking a conversation.

> ▶ **Conversation.** A *Conversation* is the iterative exchange of requirements between two parties. Information may flow back and forth several times. Therefore, a conversation ID that is embedded in the ReqIF model can be used to determine wich Conversation a specific file belongs to.

2.5.2 ReqIF Standard Attributes

The ProStep implementor forum has defined a number of standard attributes.

(i) In the following, you will only find the description of a few major standard attributes. The full list is found in the ProStep Implementor Guide, which may be purchased by ProStep.

▶ **Standard Attribute.** A standard attribute is an attribute with a well-defined name and type. Tools that honor the ProStep Implementor Guide will recognize these and handle them in a special way, typically saving the user some configuration effort.

Many existing tools already have special attributes, most notably for ID and requirements text. By providing standard names in a ReqIF file, importing tools can recognize these attribute and map them to their standard attributes. For example, the standard attribute name for the requirements text is *ReqIF.Text*. IBM Rational DOORS, for instance, would map it to "Object Text", PTC Integrity to "Text" and Visure IRQA to "Description", as those are the standard attributes in those respective tools.

Here is a list of the more notable standard attributes that apply to *SpecObjects*. The data type is shown in parentheses. The full list is found in the ProStep implementor guide:

ReqIF.Text (XHTML). Holds the actual requirements text.

ReqIF.ForeignID (String). Holds the human-readable ID from the source tool.

ReqIF.Prefix (String): Some tools use a prefix to the human-readable ID, to make it unique within the model.

ReqIF.ChapterName (XHTML). Holds the name of a Chapter.

There are many more standard attributes, concerned with timestamps, users and the like. Also note that there is another set of standard attributes for *Specifications*.

As ReqIF Studio supports ReqIF natively, there is no real need for treating any of these standard attributes in a special way, as all attributes are fundamentally equal. However, there are two exceptions:

First, attribute names starting with the prefix *ReqIF.* are rendered slightly differently in the Specification Editor: In the column headings, the prefix is stripped off and the name is rendered in blue.

Second, the column configuration dialog allows the creation of a UNIFIED COLUMN. This column allows *ReqIF.Text* and *ReqIF.ChapterName* to be shown in the same column, similar to the way IBM Rational DOORS does it.

3. Tutorial

3.1 Basic Concepts

In this tutorial, we will use the ReqIF terminology, which can be confusing. Therefore, please familiarize yourself with the terminology first (Section 2.4).

> In ReqIF terminology, a requirement is called *SpecObject*, a link is a *SpecRelation*, and the document view consists of *SpecHierarchies*. Confused? Then please have a look at Section 2.4, where the terminology is described.

3.2 Tutorial 1: Creating a Basic ReqIF Model

In this section, we will build a ReqIF model from scratch, step by step.

3.2.1 Install ReqIF Studio

The easiest way for installing ReqIF Studio is downloading ReqIF Studio[1]. This is a standalone-application that is based on Eclipse RMF, combined with some enhancements.

---

[1]https://reqif.academy

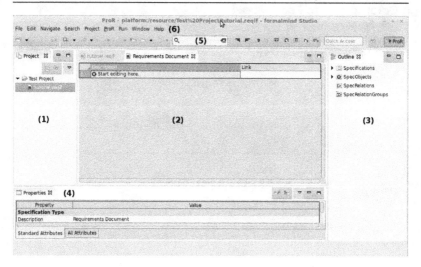

Figure 3.1: The ReqIF Studio user interface

Alternatively, you can install RMF in any Eclipse-Installation via its update site (listed on the RMF Download page[2]). This is recommended for advanced users only who need to integrate RMF with other Eclipse-based components.

ⓘ   The installation is described in detail in Section 7.2.2.

3.2.2 Create the Model

- If you do not already have one, create a new *project*: Select FILE | NEW | PROJECT;
- Create the ReqIF model by selecting FILE | NEW | REQIF10 MODEL;
- Select the project and name the file "tutorial.reqif". Click FINISH;
- Upon completion, the model will be opened, as well as the one and only SPECIFICATION contained in this model.

After this, your window should look more or less as shown in Figure 3.1.

You will see your ReqIF file in the PROJECT EXPLORER window (1).

The SPECIFICATION EDITOR (2) shows your *Specifications*.

―――――――――――――
[2]https://www.eclipse.org/rmf/download.php

In the Specification Editor, you see the *SpecObjects* that exist in this Specification. There is currently only one, with the description "Start editing here".

The OUTLINE (3) has four folders:

Specifications. Shows the Specifications in the ReqIF. You can expand the tree to expose the hierarchy of SpecObjects in the ReqIF model.

SpecObjects. Shows all SpecObjects in the ReqIF model as a flat list. Keep in mind that SpecObjects in Specifications are references. In contrast, this folder shows all SpecObjects created for the ReqIF model, whether or not they are referenced.

SpecRelations. Shows all SpecRelations in the ReqIF as a flat list. For now, we will ignore SpecRelations.

SpecRelationsGroups. These are special constructs that can be used for grouping SpecRelations with the same source and target.

The properties of a selected *SpecElement* are shown in the PROPERTIES VIEW (4). As the only SpecObject in the model is selected, we see its *SpecType* ("Requirements Type") and its only *Attribute* ("Description") with the value "Start editing here." There are two tabs STANDARD ATTRIBUTES and ALL ATTRIBUTES at the bottom of the PROPERTIES VIEW. The STANDARD ATTRIBUTES tab shows you all standard attributes of the selected element. ALL ATTRIBUTES shows all existing ReqIF attributes of the selected element.

Above the main working windows it the tool bar (5) and, at the very top, the menu bar (6).

3.2.3 Customizing the SpecType

To get familiar with the tool, we will:

- Add two more attributes to the SpecObjectType called "ID" and "Owner" and
- We will show those *Attributes* in the *Specification*

The results of this are shown in Figure 3.2.

To add new attributes, we open the DATATYPE CONFIGURATION dialog with STUDIO | DATATYPE CONFIGURATION. Alternatively you can also click on ℾ in the Tool Bar.

The resulting dialog box has two folders in the upper pane:

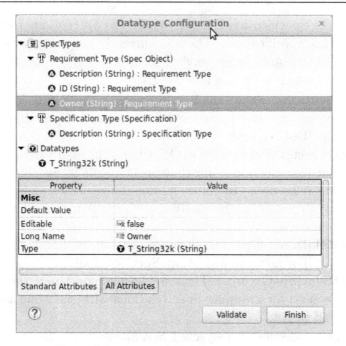

Figure 3.2: Datatype Configuration Dialog

one for *SpecTypes* and one for *Datatypes*. Currently, there is only one Datatype "T_String32k" and two SpecTypes, one called "Requirements Type" with the attribute "Description" and one called "Specification Type" with the attribute "Description".

In the lower pane are the details in regards to each attribute.

We add more Attributes to "Requirements Type" by right-clicking it and selecting NEW CHILD | ATTRIBUTE DEFINITION STRING. This will create a new element. Upon selecting it, we can rename it and tailor the details. Double-click on the "Long Name" variable and type in "ID". Change the Type by double-clicking the field and choosing "T_String32k" from the dropdown menu. Repeat the process but this time change the "Long Name" to "Owner". In the end, the dialog should look as shown in Figure 3.2.

Upon closing the dialog, little will have changed - the Specification still shows just two columns, Description and Link. However, if you select the requirement, you will see the new Properties (ID and Owner) in the Property view.

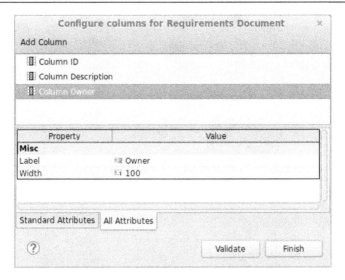

Figure 3.3: Column Configuration

3.2.4 Showing the New Attributes

To show the new Attributes in the Specification, we have to configure the columns shown in the SPECIFICATION EDITOR. We do this by selecting STUDIO | COLUMN CONFIGURATION. You can also click on ▦ in the Tool Bar.

The resulting Dialog shows one entry, "Description" for the one and only Column of the Specification. In the "Value" column double click on "Description to choose it and replace it with "ID".

By clicking on the "Add Column" icon at the top of the dialog, create a new column and name it "Description". In this view, the columns can be dragged and dropped to change their order as desired.

The resulting window is shown in Figure 3.3.

ⓘ Note that you have to provide free text for the columns for the same reason that we used free text for the "Labels" earlier: This way we can easily match multiple SpecObjects of different types.

You can actually adjust the width of the columns simply by dragging the column headers.

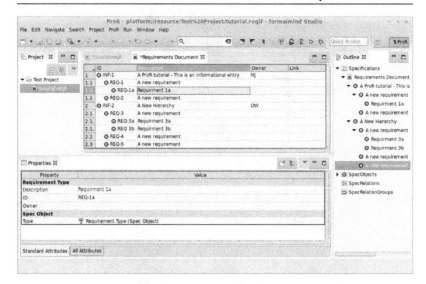

Figure 3.4: Adding SpecObjects

3.2.5 Adding new SpecObjects

Now we can finally add *SpecObjects* by right-clicking on a row in the Specification View. In the context-menu, there are two submenus: NEW CHILD and NEW SIBLING.

In both menus, there are three entries SPEC HIERARCHY, SPECOBJECT and SPECOBJECT (REQUIREMENT TYPE). Some background is needed here:

We said before that Specifications contain references to SpecObjects. A SPECHIERARCHY is the wrapper that allows the hierarchical structure and that points to the referenced SpecObject. Usually, we don't have to be concerned with them. Therefore the second option: If selected, a new SpecHierarchy is created and associated with a new SpecObject, which in turn is set immediately to the given *SpecType*. If we had more than just one SpecType (besides "Requirements Type"), there would be an entry for each SpecType in the context menu.

To continue the exercise, select the NEW CHILD | SPECOBJECT (REQUIREMENT TYPE). Now we have two SpecObjects. The original is numbered on the far left-hand side of the pane with a "1". The second one, the child, is numbered "1.1". Now we should change the ID's of each entry. Click in the cell of the column "ID" (in row 1) and type in INF-1. Under Description,

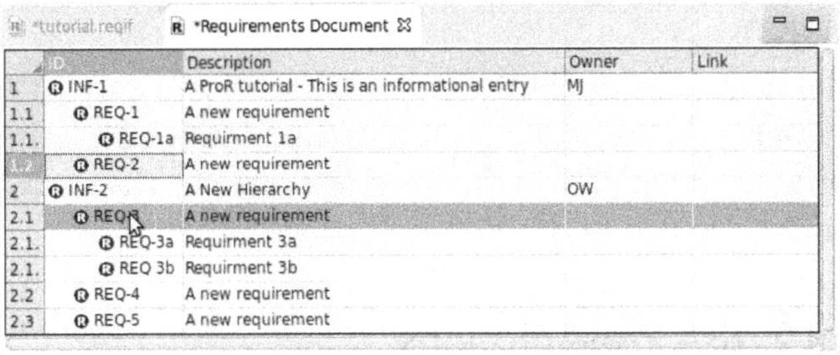

Figure 3.5: Drag and Drop

type "A ReqIF tutorial." For the second, change the ID to REQ-1 and "Learn how to create a new requirement" in the "Description" column.

Feel free to add a few more rows and or even new structures. Yours should look somethinig similar to Figure 3.4.

3.2.6 Rearranging Elements

SpecObjects can be reordered by using drag and drop. This works both in the SPECIFICATION VIEW and the OUTLINE VIEW.

You can drag and drop a SpecObject as a sibling or a child. The highlighting feedback will enable you to see what you're moving and where to. For instance, if you are dragging a SpecObject over another one, the entire cell will be highlighted. This means, that the SpecObject will be assigned as a child to the dropped SpecObject.

If you are dragging a SpecObject between two rows, you also get visual feedback on whether the SpecObject will be assigned as a sibling.

Figure 3.5 shows drag and drop in action.

You can also move elements by using cut and paste. Pasting will insert an element as a child.

3.2.7 Export Specification as HTML

If you want to export your Specification as HTML, open the Specification you would like to export and initiate printing FILE | PRINT.... The HTML representation is generated and opened in your system's web browser.

3.2.8   Conclusion

Quite an achievement—but there's still a bit of a way to go. One improvement we can make is simplifying data entry. Another is improving the visibility of the descriptions. In the next part of the tutorial, we will address these issues.

3.3   Tutorial 2: Use Presentations

We will continue where we left off at the end of Tutorial 1 and we will assume that you have ReqIF Studio open with a model identical or similar to the one we created earlier.

In this tutorial we will introduce *Presentations*. Presentations are Eclipse Plug-Ins that extend the functionality of ReqIF Studio. Specifically:

- Presentations can change the way Attributes are rendered in the Specification,
- Presentations can change the way Attributes are edited in the Specification and
- Presentations can perform tasks in the background.

ReqIF Studio comes with a number of standard presentations that we will introduce in this tutorial.

3.3.1   ID Presentation

It would be nice if every SpecObject had its own unique ID. Actually, they do: The unique ID is shown in the ALL ATTRIBUTES tab of the PROPERTY VIEW, if a SpecObject is selected. But that ID is meant for machines and is not practical.

The ID Presentation allows the automatic creation of more user-friendly IDs. Let's create one.

Remember that Presentations are associated with *Datatypes*, not *Attributes*. Thus, we first have to create a new Datatype called "T_ID". We then associate that Datatype with the Attribute "ID". We described this process in the first tutorial. Figure 3.6 shows the configuration dialog, when all is done.

The next step is the association of the Datatype with the Presentation.

We open the Presentation Configuration and create a new Presentation from the dropdown menu SELECT ACTION..., of type "Id" Presentation. We associate it with the newly created Datatype. After configuration, it would look as shown in Figure 3.7.

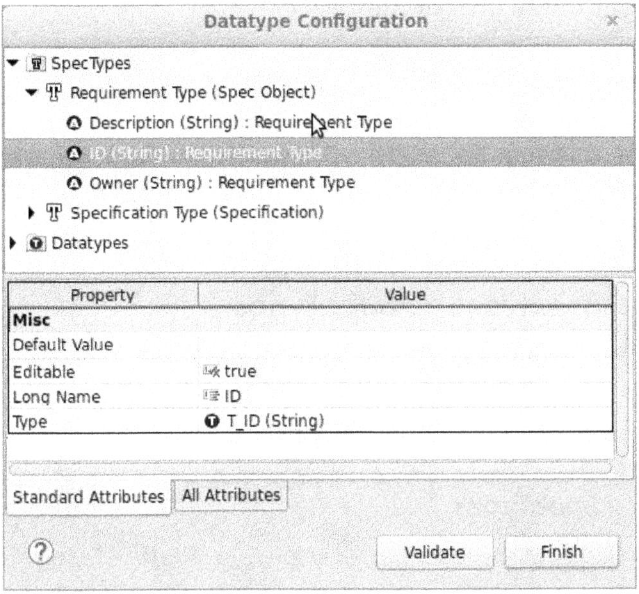

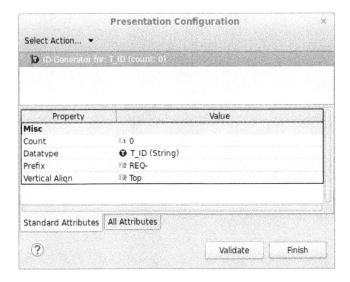

Figure 3.6: Datatype Configuration Dialog

Figure 3.7: Configuration of the ID Presentation

Note that you can adjust the prefix, count and the vertical alignment of the presentation.

> At this point, the Presentation does not yet check for duplicates. It simply grabs a new value from count, increments it and uses it. Also, existing values are never overwritten.

3.4   Tutorial 3: Advanced SpecTypes

So far, we have a model with only one SpecObjectType. In this tutorial, we will show how we can work with multiple SpecTypes, and we will introduce other SpecTypes.

3.4.1   Multiple SpecTypes

The first entry in our Specification ("A ReqIF Tutorial") isn't really a requirement. Thus, it doesn't need an ID or an owner, and it would be nice to highlight it somehow. For highlighting, we have the HEADLINE PRESENTATION. We will:

- Create a new *SpecType* for headlines.
- Create a new *Datatype* that will be used for the headline content.
- Associate that Datatype with the HEADLINE PRESENTATION.

By selecting STUDIO | DATATYPE CONFIGURATION, we open the dialog where we can create new SpecTypes and Datatypes. For the first time, we create a new SpecType by right-clicking on SPECTYPES. One of the entries in the child menu is SPECOBJECT TYPE.

Once created, we select it and rename as "Headline Type" in the PROPERTY PANE.

Then we give it a new Attribute called "Description" by right-clicking it and selecting STRING.

> It is important that we call it "Description". This matches the Attribute name from "Requirement Type". By using the same name, we ensure that the Attributes **appear in the same column**, even though they are different Attributes from different SpecTypes.

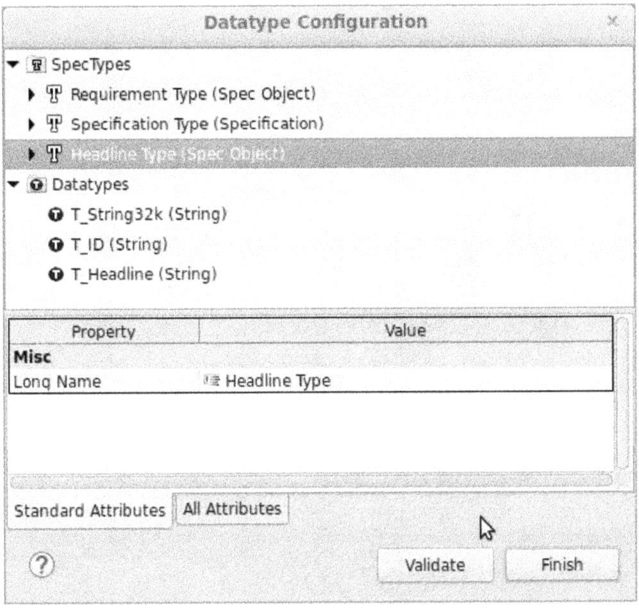

Figure 3.8: Datatype Configuration for the Headline Presentation

We do not set the type yet, as we need to create a new Datatype. We do this, as before, by right-clicking on the DATA-TYPES folder in the upper pane. Create a child of type DEFINITION STRING. Call it "T_Headline" and set the length to 50. Now we can go back to the "Description" Attribute (in the upper pane) and set the type to T_Headline, which is now available from the dropdown.

When all this is done, the resulting configuration should look as shown in Figure 3.8.

You can change the type of a SpecObject by selecting it and changing it in the PROPERTIES VIEW. Please note that currently all existing values are lost when changing the type.

Note the following:

- For SpecObjects of this SpecType, the columns "ID" and "Owner" are now empty and cannot be edited.
- Note how the PROPERTY VIEW changes as you select SpecObjects of different SpecTypes.
- Right-clicking on a row now shows one more option for child/sibling creation: A new entry of type "Headline Type".
- At this point, the description of the headline is not yet

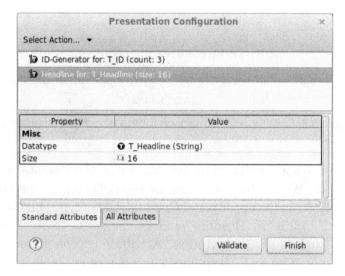

	ID	Description	Owner	Link
1	⊙	**A ProR Tutorial**		
1.1	⊗ REQ-1	A new requirement		
1.1.1	⊗ REQ-3a	Requirment 3a		0 ▷⊗▷ 1
1.1.2	⊗ REQ-1a	Requirment 1a		1 ▷⊗▷ 0
1.2	⊗ REQ-5	A new requirement		
2	⊗ INF-2	A New Hierarchy	OW	
2.1	⊗ REQ-3	A new requirement		
2.1.1	⊗ REQ 3b	Requirment 3b		
2.2	⊗ REQ-4	A new requirement		
2.2.1	⊗ REQ-2	A new requirement		
2.3	⊗ REQ-3a	Requirment 3a		0 ▷⊗▷ 1

Figure 3.9: Activated Headline Configuration

Figure 3.10: Presentation Configuration for Headline

formatted, as we have not activated the Presentation yet.

Last, we will create a HEADLINE PRESENTATION and activate it for the type "T_Headline". This is done via the PRESENTATION CONFIGURATION, as before. The configuration allows you to change the font size of the headline in the "Size" property. The presentation configuration is shown in Figure 3.10.

After all the changes, the Specification should look as shown in Figure 3.9. Note that the formatting is also applied in the PROPERTIES VIEW.

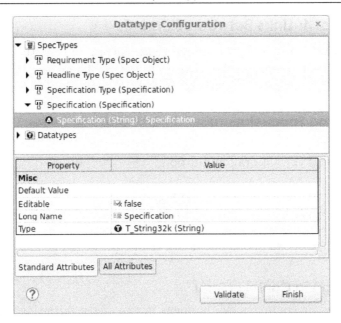

Figure 3.11: Creating a New SpecType

3.4.2 Other SpecTypes

You may have noticed in the DATATYPE CONFIGURATION DI-ALOG, that right-clicking on SPECTYPES offered more options, besides SPECOBJECT TYPE. A number of Elements can have Attributes, not just SpecObjects.

We will now create a *SpecificationType* and assign it to our Specification.

Try to create a SpecificationType and configure it as shown in Figure 3.11:

Next, we will assign this type to the one Specification that we have. To do this we select the Specification in the OUTLINE VIEW (first element in the Folder SPECIFICATIONS). That will show the Specification's properties in the PROPERTIES VIEW. The TYPE property is empty. We select "Specification Type" from the dropdown.

As soon as it is selected, the Attribute "Description" will appear in the Properties View, as now the Specification has an attribute of that name. If we set it to a meaningful name, the label in the Outline View will change as well.

3.5 Tutorial 4: Links Between Elements

A central feature of professional requirements tools is the ability
to connect requirements with each other. These are typically
called links, traces or relations. In ReqIF, these are *SpecRelations*.

3.5.1 Creating SpecRelations

There are two ways of creating SpecRelations: (1) via the context
menu and (2) via drag and drop.

> (i) We recommend to use the context menu for linking. It
>   works even if source and target are not visible, it allows
>   n:m linking, and it allows for the assignment of a SpecType
>   to the newly created SpecRelations in one step.

3.5.2 Linking Via Context Menu

Linking via context menu happens in two steps: initiating linking
and completing linking.

Linking is initiated by right-clicking on one SpecObject, or a
selection of SpecObjects. The context menu contains the option
INITIATE LINKING, with a number in parentheses. The number
indicates the count of affected SpecObjects.

Linking can only be completed if it has been initiated. In
that case, right-clicking on a single SpecObject or a selection
of SpecObjects will show two more entries in the context menu.
These are COMPLETE LINKING TO SELECTION and COMPLETE
LINKING FROM SELECTION. It will also indicate in parentheses
with how many SpecObjects the linking had been initialized.

Each of these entries has a submenu, listing all SpecTypes for
SpecRelations. By selecting the appropriate option, SpecRela-
tions will be created between the two sets of SpecObjects. The
SpecRelations will have the selected SpecType.

3.5.3 Linking Via Drag and Drop

SpecRelations are also be created by "Link-Dragging". This is
platform specific:

Linux. Dragging with Ctrl-Shift.

Mac. Hold down OPTION and APPLE/COMMAND keys while
     dragging.

Windows. Dragging with Alt.

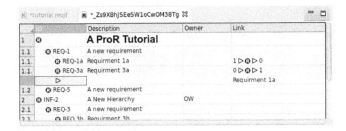

Figure 3.12: Showing Links in the GUI

3.5.4 SpecRelations in the User Interface

After creating SpecRelations, the right-most column (LINK) in the SPECIFICATION EDITOR, has content. It summarizes the number of incoming and outgoing SpecRelations. The number to the left of the triangle is incoming links, the other, outgoing links (see Figure 3.12).

Showing SpecRelations **for a single SpecObject** can be switched on or off by double-clicking on the Link cell.

Showing SpecRelations **for all SpecObjects** can be switched on or off with the little triangle icon in the toolbar ▷.

As SpecRelations can have Attributes, these are shown in the corresponding column, if the column name matches the Attribute name. Selecting the row of a SpecRelation will show all its Attributes in the PROPERTIES VIEW.

The LINK cell of a SpecRelation shows the label of the link target of that SpecRelation. Selecting it will show the link target's Attributes in the PROPERTIES VIEW (instead of the SpecRelation's Attributes, as for all other cells).

ⓘ Selecting the LINK column of a SpecRelation allows the link target to be quickly inspected.

Figure 3.12 shows a Specification where REQ-1a and REQ-3a are linked.

3.5.5 Following SpecRelations

It is possible to navigate along SpecRelations. To do so, make the links visible, as described in Section 3.5.4. Double-clicking on the label of the link target will open the appropriate Specification and select the SpecObject.

As Specifications contain references to SpecObjects, there are two other situations that can occur:

The target SpecObject is not used in any Specification. In that situation, double-clicking will have no effect. But clicking on the label will show the target SpecObject's attributes in the Properties View, where they can be inspected and edited.

The target SpecObject is referenced multiple times. In that case, a menu will open to show all places where the SpecObject is used. The user can select the place to navigate to.

3.5.6 SpecRelations in the Outline View

The OUTLINE VIEW has a folder showing all SpecRelations. This folder is shown only when the ReqIF editor (Section 7.3.2) is active.

4. Presentations

ReqIF Studio has an extension mechanism that allows custom rendering, custom editing and automatic modifications to the requirements model. These extensions are called *presentations*.

Presentations can be created and configured via STUDIO | PRESENTATION CONFIGURATION... or the icon 🎭 in the toolbar. Launching it will show the dialog shown in Figure 4.1. Initially, the dialog will be empty. The dialog in the figure shows two presentation configurations.

Presentations are specific for a model, and its configuration is also stored in the requirements model.

ReqIF Studio ships with a small set of standard presentations. Additional presentations can be installed into ReqIF Studio.

> Note that presentations are specific to ReqIF Studio, not to ReqIF. This means that other tools will simply ignore presentations. Also note that the behavior of the tool is unpredictable if a presentation used by a model is not installed in ReqIF Studio.

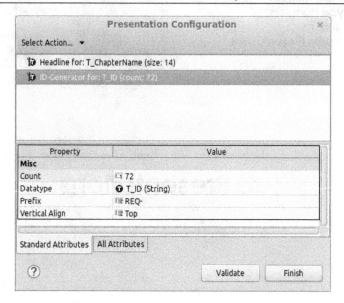

Figure 4.1: The presentation dialog with two configured presentations

4.1 Working with Presentations

All presentations are configured in the same way. To configure a presentation for the current model, first open the presentation configuration dialog as described above.

Initially, the dialog is empty. You can add new presentations using the SELECT ACTION... dropdown. It will list all built-in and installed presentations. Upon selecting an entry, it will be added to the list below.

> ⓘ It is possible (and often useful) to add the same presenta-tion multiple times. For instance, one could add multiple ID generation presentations for different types of elements (with correspondingly different prefixes).

Selecting a presentation in the upper pane will show its con-figuration parameters in the lower pane. In Figure 4.1, the ID-Generator is selected, and the lower pane shows its four configu-ration parameters.

All presentations have a configuration parameter DATATYPE. Typically, the datatype determines whether a presentation is applied to an element or not.

> (i) If you want a presentation to be applied to a dedicated
> *Attribute* (rather than *Datatype*, then simply create a
> specific datatype for that attribute. And conversely, you
> can reuse a single presentation for multiple attributes by
> using the same datatype for all relevant Attributes.

The order of entries sometimes (but rarely) matters. Presentations can be reordered using drag and drop.

Last, to delete a presentation, select DELETE from the context menu by right-clicking.

4.2 Default Datatype Handlers

Sometimes, it is desirable to use a presentation as the default for rendering (and editing) a specific datatype. For example, the open source RMF can not render formatted (XHTML) text and instead shows a simplification in plain text. But ReqIF Studio offers the RTF presentation that allows rich rendering and editing. Thus, it would be nice if XHTML datatypes would always be rendered using the RTF presentation, if installed.

This is possible. And in fact, presentations can request to be used as default handlers. If such a presentation is installed, it will automatically take over from the default.

Users can configure and override this. To do so, go to WINDOW | PREFERENCES | REQIF | DEFAULT PRESENTATIONS. The resulting dialog is shown in Figure 4.2.

For each of the standard ReqIF datatypes, a handler can be chosen. The default is NONE. The following entries are available:

None. This is the default and implies that the build-in renderer is used. Upon starting the tool, ReqIF Studio will check whether a new presentation has been installed that requests to act as the default handler for that datatype. If such a presentation is found, it will be set as the handler.

Use Built-in. This forces the built-in handler to be used. Even if an installed presentation requests to be the handler, the built-in handler will continue to be used.

List of installed presentations. The remaining entries list all installed presentations. Note that the dialog does not filter the matching types. I.e. even though the RTF presentation is only applicable for XHTML, it is shown in the dropdown for all datatypes.

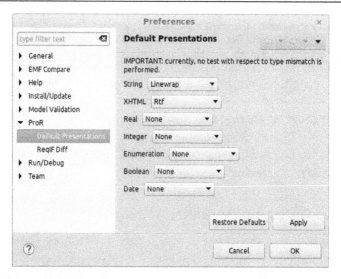

Figure 4.2: The preference dialog for handling default presentations

> Please make sure that you only set datatype handlers of the correct type. Also note that there is no access to the configuration parameters of default handlers. Therefore, this mechanism makes only sense for presentations that do not require any additional configuration.

4.3 Built-in Presentations

The following presentations are part of the Eclipse RMF project and are therefore open source.

4.3.1 ID Generator Presentation

This presentation automatically generates user-friendly IDs, consisting of a prefix and a number, e.g. "REQ-12". The configuration parameters are shown in Figure 4.2.

> Attributes to which this presentation applies are read-only and cannot be edited manually any more (as long as the presentation is active).

The parameters are:

Count. The counter position. When a new ID is created, it will be incremented by one. Changing it allows the user to start or continue with a different number.

Datatype. The presentation will be applied to all attributes with
this datatype. Must by of type *String*.

Prefix. The prefix to the number. Note that changing this will
only modify newly created IDs, not those already generated.

Vertical align. Allows to adjust how the text shall be rendered
in the cell.

Currently, the presentation does not check whether duplicate IDs exist!

4.3.2 Headline Presentation

This presentation renders the content of a cell boldface in a large
font. This can be useful if you want to format text to stand out
(e.g. a headline), without having to resort to XHTML.

The parameters are:

Datatype. The presentation will be applied to all attributes with
this datatype. Must by of type *String*.

Size. The size of the text in point.

4.3.3 Linewrap

This presentation wraps text at word boundaries, essentially what
one would expect anyway. The built-in renderer breaks the text
anywhere, including in the middle of words.

This presentation is usually set as the default presentation.

Regular users can just ignore this presentation. It has
been created for developers to understand the presentation
mechanism.

4.4 Built-in ReqIF Studio Presentations

The following presentations are part of ReqIF Studio and Essentials. They are freely available.

4.4.1 Rich Text Formatting (RTF)

The RTF presentation requires Java 7 or better from
Oracle to work.

Description	Source	Target	Link
1	® Source			0 ▷ ® ▷ 1
	▷		⚠	Target
2	® Target			1 ▷ ® ▷ 0

Figure 4.3: The change management indicates that the link target has changed

The RTF presentation renders attributes of type XHTML formatted, as intended. It also provides a rich text editor.

> (i) The RTF presentation registers itself as the default handler when installed. Therefore, this presentation is rarely used explicitly. As a regular user, just ignore it: It will activate automatically wherever needed.

4.4.2   Change Management

This presentation tracks changes in the source and target of a *SpecRelation*. Therefore, it is a useful extension that helps users to verify whether a relationship is still valid after a change. How this works in practice is shown in Figure 4.3:

In the figure, two SpecObjects are shown that are linked by a SpecRelation. The SpecRelation is unfolded. It has two attributes, *Source* and *Target* (not to be confused with the source and target of the SpecRelation). As can be seen, the attribute *Target* shows an exclamation mark. This indicates that the target has changed, since it was inspected last time.

Now the user can inspect the changes and ensure that the link still makes sense. Once this is done, the flag is reset by double-clicking it.

> (i) The change flag can be toggled by double-clicking it. This allows the flag to be reset, and also to mark objects for inspection at a later time.

If the user would now make a change to the source or target SpecObject of the SpecRelation, the corresponding flag on the SpecRelation would be activated again.

Setting up the Datatypes

For the presentation to work, the datatypes have to be set up correctly. Specifically:

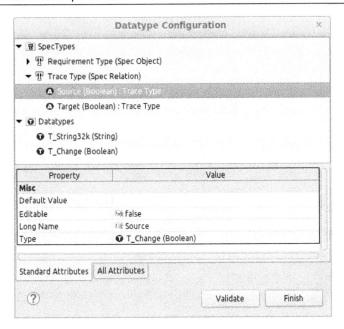

Figure 4.4: Configuration of the datatypes for change management

- There must be a Boolean datatype for the flags.
- The SpecRelation must have two boolean attribute, using the previously mentioned datatype.

How such a configuration would look like is shown in Figure 4.4.

ⓘ It can be useful to also add two columns for the change flags, as shown in Figure 4.3.

Configuring the Presentation

The presentation itself has the following four parameters. Figure 4.5 shows a properly configured presentation for the previously shown datatypes:

Datatype. Here you have to provide the Boolean datatype that has been used for the flags. Must by of type *Boolean.*

Link Relation Type. Select the SpecRelationType that holds the change flags from the dropdown.

Source Status. The attribute from the SpecRelationType that tracks the source object.

Target Status. The attribute from the SpecRelationType that tracks the target object.

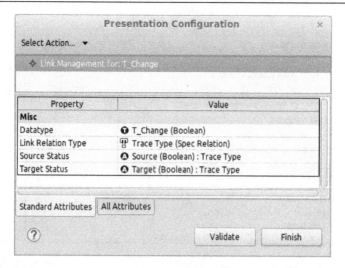

Figure 4.5: Configuration of the presentation for change management

4.4.3 Keyword Highlighting (Glossary)

In this section, we describe two presentations, *Keyword* and *Highlight*, which work hand-in-hand.

The highlight presentation allows the highlighting of certain keywords in the requirements text.

The keyword presentation determines where the keywords are coming from. It is also possible to write new presentations that pull the keywords from a different source, e.g. a data dictionary or a data model.

> At this point, highlighting works only with plain text requirements (not XHTML). Further, keywords must be marked by the user with square brackets.

Setting up the Datatypes

We start with the glossary. We recommend to set up a dedicated *SpecObjectType* for glossary terms, but this is not strictly necessary. Rather, it is necessary to have a dedicated attribute. Figure 4.6 shows a glossary, with one term selected and shown in the Properties View.

As is apparent in the Properties View, a glossary term is of type *Glossary Type* (which we created for this purpose). The attribute *Term* is the one that matters. This attribute will be

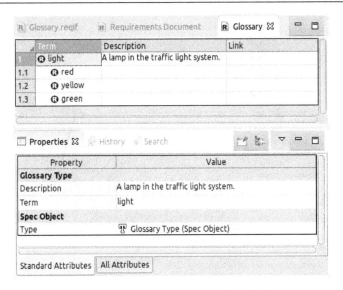

Figure 4.6: A Glossary (top), with one term selected and shown in the Properties View (bottom)

used for the glossary management.

Next we want to use this glossary to produce highlighting as shown in Figure 4.7. Square brackets are used to mark glossary terms. This is done to prevent words to be highlighted that are glossary terms, but used in a different context. For instance, if the controller case shall be painted in green, this would not refer to the glossary term "green", which applies to the light (not the case).

In the figure, the upper pane is in edit mode, the lower pane is not. In both, the term "green" has been highlighted in green, as it appears in the glossary. Also, in both "yelow" is shown in red: it is spelled incorrectly, and therefore does not match the glossary term "yellow".

Last, the term "red" is underlined, but only in edit mode: This is a hint for users (while they edit), that they may want to highlight the term, as there is a matching one in the glossary.

Configuring the Presentation

Two activate the glossary, two presentations must be configured.

> The order of the presentations matters: the *Highlight* presentation must appear before the *Keyword* presentation.

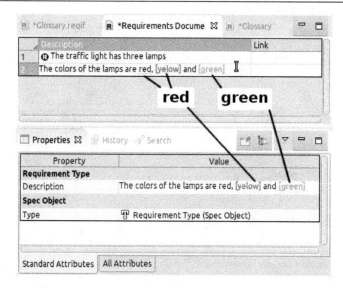

Figure 4.7: The terms are now highlighted when surrounded by square brackets. If the term is not found, the highlighting is red. Further, in edit mode (upper pane), matching terms that are not marked as such are underlined in red.

Also, you may need to close and reopen the model.

The highlight presentation has only one parameter. It defines which datatypes shall be observed for color highlighting:

Datatype. The datatype for which rendering shall be activated. This is **not** the glossary type, but, in this case, T_STRING32.

The keyword presentation creates the connection between glossary and requirements text. It has the following four parameters:

Color. The highlight color. If left empty, blue is used. Another color can be defined, consisting of three comma-separated numbers, representing red, green and blue, on a scale from 0-255. E.g. 0,255,0 for green.

Datatype. The datatype for which rendering shall be activated. This the same that has been selected in teh highlight presentation.

Keywords. The attribute to be used for retrieving keywords.

Priority. It is possible to provide multiple Keyword presentations, e.g. for using different colors. If a keyword exists in more than one glossary, then the priority determines which presentation (and therefore, which color) is being used.

4.5 Other Presentations

Here you find a non-exhaustive list of external presentations that we are aware of.

4.5.1 Rodin Integration Presentation

The University of Düsseldorf maintains a presentation for traceability between Event-B models and requirements.

ⓘ See: http://wiki.event-b.org/index.php/ProR

4.5.2 EMF Integration Presentation (UML/SysML)

The openETCS project maintains a presentation for traceability between any EMF model and requirements. This has been applied specifically for the Eclipse Papyrus component, allowing traceability between UML and SysML models.

ⓘ See: https://github.com/openETCS/toolchain/wiki/User-Documentation

Axiom
Binom
Consequent
Deduct

5. Components

In addition to Presentation (Chapter 4), there are more comprehensive components that typically consist of a number of elements to provide more sophisticated functionality. This chapter describes those components created by Formal Mind.

> (i) Components can be downloaded from https://reqif.academy. Note that most components described here are premium content that requires a paid membership.

Component Names.
The components are named using terms from the mathematical discipline of Logic, which is typically loosely connected to the task of the component. A short explanation of the term is usually provided in the respective chapter. The names are chosen to create an alphabetical order, reflecting the time of creation.

5.1 Axiom

The requirements exchange component *Axiom* allows you to exchange requirements according to the HIS process[1]. The HIS

---

[1] http://formalmind.com/de/blog/his-exchange-process-requirements-all-you-ever-wanted-know

process was developed by the automotive industry to exchange requirements between manufacturer (OEM) and supplier.

> (i) The exchange component *Axiom* is not available for free. You need to purchase a license from Formal Mind and install it with the license manager.

Typically, an OEM creates a requirements specification for a supplier to review. The supplier then comments the specification, accepting or rejecting individual requirements. This workflow is visualized in Figure 5.1 (which is documented in the ReqIF specification).

In a more sophisticated scenario, the OEM may request a system specification that outlines how the requirements are being realized. In such an exchange scenario, the supplier would send the system specification back to the OEM, including a traceability between requirements specification and system specification.

Generally, we have to distinguish between an initial exchange, during which new information is transmitted, and subsequent exchanges, during which information is updated.

With an exchange (as opposed to an import), elements are selectively added and/or updated. Before describing the wizards in detail, we need to describe some concepts.

> ▶ **Axiom.** In logic, an axiom is a starting point of reasoning. An invalid or contradicting axiom can falsify a complete chain of reasoning. The Axiom component ensures that two parties have a common foundation for their work.

5.1.1 Concepts

The objective of the Exchange is to **selectively update requirements, specifications and links**. Updating can mean adding, changing and removing elements. This is best visualized with Figure 5.1.

Partner 1 starts by creating a requirements export with RM-Tool A. This export is filtered both *vertically* (only a subset of SpecObjects is exported) and *horizontally* (not all attributes are exported).

Partner 2 processes the requirements by importing (first time) or merging them (subsequently). Partner 2 can augment the

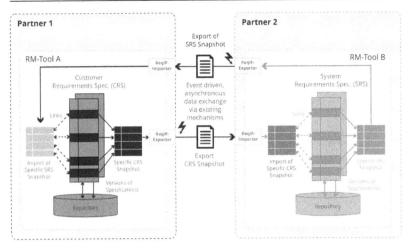

Figure 5.1: Visualization of a typical requirements exchange. (Source: (Jastram, 2014), with friendly permission.)

requirements both vertically (inserting more elements) or horizontally (adding more attributes).

Eventually, Partner 2 will provide feedback by creating an export. Partner 1 probably already created attributes for this purpose, e.g. *Supplier Status* or *Supplier Comment*. Upon importing, Partner 1 would only update those attributes.

Likewise, if Partner 1 changes their requirements by modifying SpecObjects or adding new ones, they can simply produce a corresponding export. The new information can be merged with the existing requirements from Partner 2, without disturbing them.

> (i) Note that the importer will **never** delete elements. If requirements are removed from specifications, then they are still present (and accessible via OUTLINE | SPECOB-JECTS). Note, however, that values of elements can and will change.

5.1.2 The Wizards

Export and import are implemented as *Wizards*. They can be triggered via the FILE | IMPORT... and FILE | EXPORT... menus, or via the context menus of the projects in the Project Explorer. This will trigger the wizard selection dialog, which lists the available

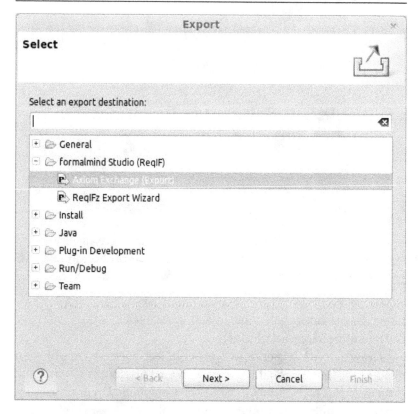

Figure 5.2: Selecting the Axiom export wizard. The import wizard is found correspondingly.

wizards by category. The Axiom wizards are found in the REQIF STUDIO (REQIF) category, as shown in Figure 5.2

The wizards are very similar: Think about an export like an import in an empty ReqIF model. Therefore, we will describe the wizard pages in the following in general terms, with subsections that describe how import and export differ.

> (i) To avoid any inconsistencies, the wizards can only be opened if all open models are saved.

Wizard Page: Project Selection

The first wizard page will only be shown if the active project cannot be determined. Otherwise it will allow you to select a project from the ones in your workspace with a dropdown.

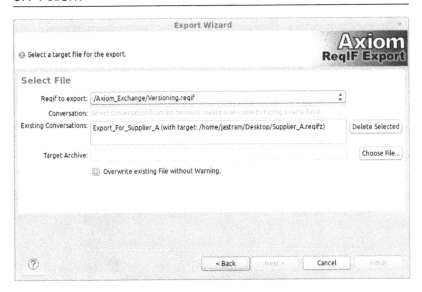

Figure 5.3: Selecting the target archive of an export

> We recommend starting the wizards via the project con-
> text menu (right-click on the project in the PROJECT
> VIEW: This way, the correct project is already prese-
> lected. If the wizard is started from the context menu of
> a ReqIF file, the source (for an export) or the target (for
> an import) is also preselected.

Wizard Page: Files and Conversations

This page requires the selection of source and target for the
exchange, as shown in Figure 5.2. The choice, including the
selection of Specifications and Attributes, can be saved as a
Conversation.

▶ **Conversation.** A conversation has two purposes. Within
Axiom, a conversation saves the configuration of an import or
export. The conversation can be restored with one click. It
can be deleted on the corresponding wizard page.

The second purpose is to store a *shared conversation id*
that allows the parties involved in an exchange to recognize
to which conversation the .reqif file belongs. Upon export,
the chosen conversation id is written into the resulting file.
Upon import, an embedded conversation id will be used to
prepopulate the import wizard with the settings used during

| the last import of the file belonging to this conversation.

If an entry is selected from EXISTING CONVERSATIONS, all other values are prepopulated.

The elements on this page for the exporter are:

ReqIF to export. This dropdown shows all ReqIF models in the selected project. Only one model at a time can be exported.

Conversation. Type the name of the Conversation here if you want to create a new one. To reuse an existing one:

Existing conversations. Conversations that have been created in the past are shown here. Selecting one will replace source and target models, and will prepopulate the values on the following pages.

Delete selected. This button will permanently remove the selected existing conversation.

Target archive. The file that will be created by the export.

Overwrite existing file without warning. The target file will be overwritten without a confirmation.

Differences for the Importer

The importer has a similar structure to the exporter, but source and target models are reversed: As the source, a .reqif file or an archive (.reqifz or .zip) has to be selected. If the source is an archive containing multiple .reqif files, the source can be selected from the IMPORT REQIF dropdown. Only one model at a time can be imported.

For the importer, the target is an existing model in the project (to be selected from a dropdown).

If the source model contains a conversation id, it will be prepopulated. If a conversation id with that name already exists, its configuration will be loaded.

> ⓘ There is no confirmation warning to overwrite a file. However, a backup is created, see Section 5.1.3.

> ⓘ The Importer will suggest to close related files before performing the import, which is recommended. If you work with large files, it is advisable to close all open editors both on import and export.

Wizard Page: Selecting Specifications

The next page allows the user to select the *Specifications* to be processed. For the Exporter, the table lists all specifications in the source, including their configured label and their internal ID. The selected specifications, including the SpecObjects they contain, will be exported. Not all attributes will be exported. This is selected on the following wizard page.

For the Importer, the labels of both, the source and the target, Specifications are shown. Also, checking a source Specification can result in two states:

New Specification. ✦ If the specification does not yet exist in the target, it will be created.

Update Specification. ✦ If the specification already exists in the target, it will be updated. This means that the requirements structure in the target is replaced with the imported structure. This can result in SpecObjects "disappearing" from the Specification. Axiom will never delete elements, and those SpecObjects can still be accessed from the outline (via the SPECOBJECTS folder).

ⓘ The importer allows to continue **without selecting a specification**. In this special case, all SpecObjects in the destination model will be updated. However, SpecObjects in the source that do not yet exist in the target will be ignored.

Wizard Page: Selecting Attributes

The next page allows the user to select the *Attributes* to be processed. For the Exporter, the table lists all SpecTypes and their Attributes in the source, including their configured label and their internal ID. The selected Attributes (and implicitly their SpecTypes) will be exported. This includes SpecTypes for SpecObjects, Specifications, SpecRelations and RelationGroups.

The Importer distinguishes between attributes that already exist (and are therefore updated ✦) and those that do not exist (and are therefore added ✦). This is shown in Figure 5.4. Like in the previous page, the Importer shows the configured labels of the source and target Attributes.

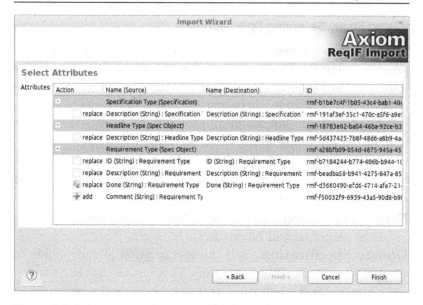

Figure 5.4: Selecting the Axiom Export Wizard. The Import Wizard is found correspondingly.

Wizard Page: Summary

Upon completion, a summary dialog is shown (Figure 5.5). It consists of three panes:

Summary pane. The top pane provides a summary of the operation, including the counts of additions, updates, etc.

Affected objects. The middle pane consists of a list of elements that were modified (or added). Selecting an element allows you to inspect it.

Property View. The bottom pane shows the full log message and the details of the element selected on the middle pane and allows for their inspection.

The export summary looks very similar, but will not contain any updates.

SpecRelations

SpecRelations (links between SpecObjects) are automatically imported or exported if the source and target SpecObjects also exist in the target (after processing the Specifications). For those SpecRelations, only the selected attributes are imported or exported.

If a SpecRelation was not exchanged because of a missing

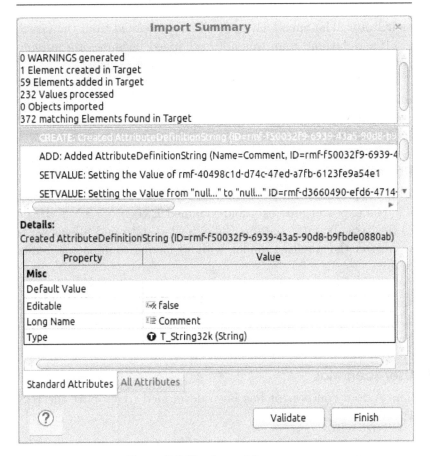

Figure 5.5: The Import Summary

source or target SpecObject, a warning will be generated.

RelationGroups

RelationGroups represent a group of SpecRelations between a source Specification and a target Specification. RelationGroups are only imported or exported if the source and target Specifications exist in the target.

Only SpecRelations existing in the target will be added to the imported or exported RelationGroups.

When importing a model, all SpecRelations existing in the target RelationGroup but not in the source RelationGroup will be removed from the target RelationGroup. Note that this only affects the association between the SpecRelation and the RealtionGroup. The SpecRelation itself is not deleted from the target.

If a RelationGroup was not exchanged because of a missing source or target Specification, a warning will be generated.

If a RelationGroup has different source or target Specifications in the source and target models, a warning will be generated. The source and target attributes of RelationGroups are not updated during an import.

5.1.3 Backups

Both, importer and exporter, create backups in the project folder.

The exporter creates a folder named EXPORT-YYYYMMD-DHHMMSS. It only contains the exported data and allows users to inspect the resulting model, without having to unpack a .reqifz archive.

The importer saves the original model, before modification through the import, in the top-level folder BACKUP. This will contain other folders, named YYYYMMDDHHMMSS, for each backup created.

5.1.4 User Scenarios

The Axiom component has been developed to support the HIS Process.

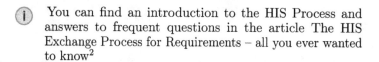

You can find an introduction to the HIS Process and answers to frequent questions in the article The HIS Exchange Process for Requirements – all you ever wanted to know[2]

5.2 Binom

Binom is a commercial-grade component for comparing ReqIF models, which seamlessly integerates into ReqIF Studio. Features of Binom include a visual, structural compare, advanced filtering, customized property view, and more.

Some Differences of ReqIF Files are not shown in the compare-view because they are meant to be different

---

[2]http://formalmind.com/en/blog/his-exchange-process-requirements-all-you-ever-wanted-know

in each ReqIF File or they are irrelevant. For example different timestamps in the "Last Change" attribute will never cause a Difference as long as the other values did not change. Also the ReqIF Headers will always be matched, though they are supposed to have different Identifiers. Last, Tool Extensions are ignored by Binom as well.

5.2.1 Getting the Compare Component

The compare component *Binom* is not available for free. You need to purchase a license from Formal Mind and install it with the license manager. Please visit the Formal Mind Online Shop at http://formalmind.com/shop.

5.2.2 Accessing Binom

Like the free version, Binom is an extension to the generic Eclipse compare tool and therefore seamlessly integrated into the Workbench. That means Binom is automatically used whenever a compare operation of two ReqIF files is triggered.

Such a compare can be initated in various ways:

- **Compare two different ReqIFs**: Select two different ReqIF Files, right-click on the selection and choose COMPARE WITH > EACH OTHER.
- **Compare a ReqIF to an earlier version**: Right-click on a ReqIF file and select COMPARE WITH > LOCAL HISTORY. In the *History View* double-click on the version you want to compare with the current version.
- **Compare two versions**: To compare two earlier versions of a ReqIF, select these versions in the *History View* and select COMPARE WITH EACH OTHER from the context menu.
- **Integration with Team Work and Version Control**: The Diff Tool is also used by Team Work Plugins like the ones described in 6.1. That means it is automatically used if ReqIFs are compared to a repository version. Simply follow the instruction in Section 6.1.2 to compare a ReqIF to a version from a repository.

5.2.3 Overview of the GUI

Figure 5.6 shows a typical result of a compare process.

The Compare View is split into two parts:

The top pane shows the structure of the comparison result as a

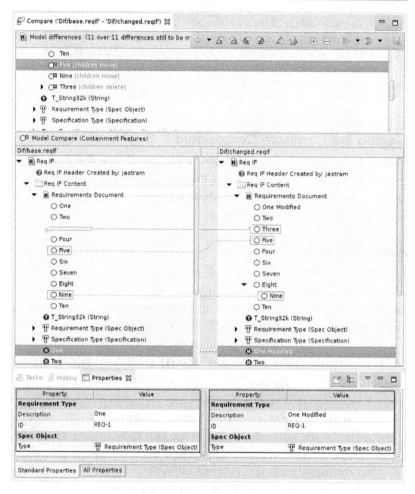

Figure 5.6: Comparing Models with Binom

summary of the differences found in the models. This pane also contains the controls to navigate through the changes an to merge them as described in Section 5.2.4.

The Lower Pane shows a side by side comparison of the models and visualizes the structural changes by connecting changed elements with lines. This pane is linked to the upper pane: By double clicking on a difference in the upper compare structure, the matching elements will be selected in the lower pane and the trees will be expanded as needed.

Additionally the existing *Properties View* is changed to provide

Figure 5.7: The Compare Toolbar

a side-by-side comparison of the two versions of a ReqIF-Element as described in Section 5.2.6.

5.2.4 Top Panel

The top pane contains a tree with all the model differences and a toolbar with buttons to navigate through the differences and to interact with them. These buttons as shown in Figure 5.7 are:

(1) Shows the number of differences still to be merged, and the number of differences filtered from the view.

(2) Allows to change the direction of consequences that are highlighted in green and red in the top panel. You can either display the consequences of a merge from left to right or right to left.

(3) Allows to merge the single, currently selected, difference either from left to right, or from right to left.

(4) Allows to merge all non conflicting differences (left to right, or right to left) at once.

(5) Allows to navigate through the differences, i.e. jumping the next or previous one.

(6) Allows to expand/collapse all differences in the top panel.

(7) Allows to change the way the differences are grouped: By default a tree structure is shown that reflects the typical structure of a ReqIF and shows all differences as they occur (as shown in Figure 5.6). By setting the grouping to *By Kind*, the differences are grouped into their kind, i.e. additions, deletions, changes, etc.

(8) Allows to filter the view. This allows you to show or hide identical elements or cascading changes (see Section 5.2.7).

(9) Allows to save the comparison model.

The difference overview shows a tree view of the match model using different indicators to highlight the differences:

- ▣ indicates a change (set/unset/move) in the left side model of the comparison.

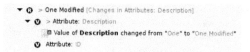

Figure 5.8: Difference in an Attribute Value

Figure 5.9: Compare View with accepted changes

- ⊞ indicates an addition in the left side model of the comparison.
- ⊟ indicates an deletion in the left side model of the comparison.
- `>` : The prefix `>` indicates, that this element has at least one child containing a difference, even if the element itself is noch changed at all.
- In case the the element is a SpecObject and some of its AttributeValues are changed, a list with the names of these Attributes is also shown as shown in Figure 5.8.

Once a difference is accepted to be merged, these indicators change to represent the merge status:

- ⊟ indicates a difference that has been merged from right to left.
- ⊟ indicates a difference that has been merged from left to right.

All merged differences will also change their color to gray as shown in Figure 5.9.

Compare of the raw XML Data.

If the upper pane shows the default view, the last node is always the match of the resources. Doubleclicking this will open a textual compare of the raw xml-files in the lower pane.

Consequences of merging a difference.

Sometimes a difference can not be applied to the other side without merging other differences too. For example imagine a SpecObject with Attributes was added on one side. This will result in more

Figure 5.10: Merge consequences are highlighted

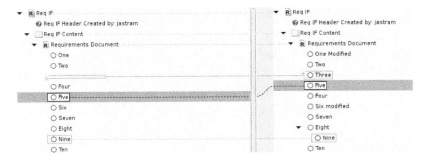

Figure 5.11: Moving and Adding Elements

than one difference to be found:

- A new SpecObject added to the ReqIF Content.
- The Type of that SpecObject is set.
- An AttributeValue is added to the SpecObject.
- The Datatype Definition of that Attribute is set.
- etc.

Some of these individual differences depend on each other and can not be merged without merging the others too. For example if you want to apply the "definition set" of the the attribute, the SpecObject has to be created and added first. Then the attribute has to be created before we can finally set the datatype definition.

Such consequences or prerequisites of a merge are highlighted with a green background in the Diff-Tree, as illustrated in Figure 5.10, and Binom will resolve them automatically.

5.2.5 Lower Pane

There are broadly two kinds changes in the structure of a Requirements Document (or Specification, in ReqIF terminology): (1) moving elements around, including in and out of hierarchies, and (2) adding (or removing) requirements. Figure 5.11 shows both.

The moving around of elements can be seen in a number of

places. For instance, the order of FIVE has changed to the position before FOUR. Likewise, for the element NINE, the hierarchy has changed, becoming a child of EIGHT (rather than a sibling).

The addition or deletion of an element can be seen with THREE, which has been added on the right side.

We use visual clues to visualize the changes. Structural changes in elements are marked by boxing them, and corresponding elements are connected by lines. Changes propagate up to the top of the hierarchy, which is the reason why the "Requirements Doucument", the "Req IF Content" and the root "Req IF" are marked with dashed lines, but not boxed. Added or deleted elements are boxed and marked with a ⁺ symbol as you can see next to the THREE in Figure 5.11.

5.2.6 Properties

While the compare Editor is active, the PROPERTIES VIEW shows a side by side comparison of the objects selected in the lower pane, as shown in Figure 5.12.

If the compare process found any differences in attributes, the corresponding labels are highlighted. In the Properties View, the model elements can be edited as usual (see Chapter 7) which is especially useful if you want to resolve merge-conflicts where accepting a difference in whole is not suitable.

> Please note that though it is possible to edit any ReqIF model through the Properties View, that does not necessarily mean the file will finally be updated. For example if you change an older version from the local history, the underlying framework will ignore any changes as this would contradict the concept of a file history.

5.2.7 Filtering

The Controls of the upper Pane provide an option to filter the difference tree:

Identical Elements hides all elements without any difference.

Cascading differences hides all differences that are a consequence of another difference. For Example if a SpecObject is deleted, all of it attributes are also deleted. While this

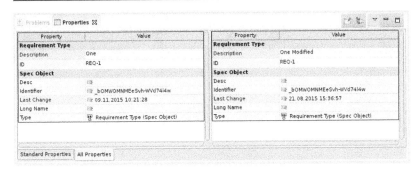

Figure 5.12: The Properties View of the Compare Window highlights attributes that have changed.

is shown as multiple differences, this is obvious and can be hidden from the difference tree.

These filters can also be defined to be active by default in the EMF Compare Preferences: PREFERENCES | EMF | FILTERS

In future releases, Binom will also offer a feature to define ReqIF-specific filters to hide certain elements or differences in specific attributes.

5.2.8 Merging

Merging differences is done by using the controls of the top panel, as shown in Figure 5.13: After selecting a difference in the upper pane you can use the controls to copy a difference from left to right or from right to left. If a change can not be merged without merging other prerequisites as described in Section 5.2.4, Binom wil automatically do so. The available operations are described in Section 5.2.4.

In the current beta version of Binom, merging is only supported for two-way comparisons. Automatically merging of all dependent differences is not yet fully supported. You might have to run a Diff-Merge process several times until a Difference is fully merged.

Any copied changes are immediately applied to the model in memory and the diff-view is updated accordingly. To save the changes, select FILE | SAVE or press Ctrl-S as usual. Also you can use Eclipses functions to undo any operation (EDIT | UNDO or CTRL-Z).

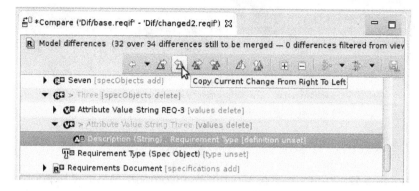

Figure 5.13: Several toolbar operations for merging exist

Resolving Conflicts

In case you have to resolve a conflict manually and copying a change in whole is not acceptable, you can use the Properties View to edit any model element as needed.

5.3 Consequent

Consequent is actually not a separate component any more. Instead, it is the build-in ReqIF validator (Section 7.3.8. There is also a stand-alone version of Consequent available.

▶ **Consequent.** Logical consequence (also Entailment) is a fundamental concept in logic, which describes the relationship between statements that holds true when one statement logically follows from one or more statements.

5.4 Deduct

Deduct is a component for creating a traceability matrix.

▶ **Traceability Matrix.** A traceability matrix is a table, used to assist in determining the completeness of a relationship by correlating any two lists using a many-to-many relationship comparison.

A traceability matrix visualizes *SpecRelations* in a grid. A SpecRelation represents the relationship between two SpecObjects, a source and a target.

Traceability matrices are used frequently in requirements management for analyzing relationships, or for spotting missing relationships or "hot spots" in the system description.

Generally, any relationship can be visualized. Practical examples include the relationship between requirements and tests, or customer requirements and system requirements (in German, Lastenheft and Pflichtenheft).

▶ **Deduct.** Deductive reasoning is the process of reasoning from one or more statements (premises) to reach a logically certain conclusion.

5.4.1 Prerequisites

Before a traceability matrix can be generated, the actual traceability has to be created: SpecRelations between SpecObjects must exists.

The axes of the traceability matrix are defined by Specifications: These determine the order of the SpecObjects. Therefore, for each of the two axes, a Specification must exist.

(i) It is perfectly acceptable to use the same Specification for both axes.

There are some special cases. In particular, SpecRelations to be shown may require SpecObjects that are missing from the axes. There are configuration options for these scenarios, described in Section 5.4.5.

5.4.2 Launching Deduct

Deduct can be launched in various ways:

Via the menu. STUDIO | TRACEABILITY MATRIX. Note that one element in the model must be selected.

Via the toolbar. using ⊞). Note that one element in the model must be selected.

As a wizard. Right-click on a ReqIF file in the project view. From the context menu, select EXPORT... | REQIF STUDIO | REQIF MATRIX EXPORT. Using this option does not require the file to be opened. Also, if the opened file has unsaved changes, these will not be considered.

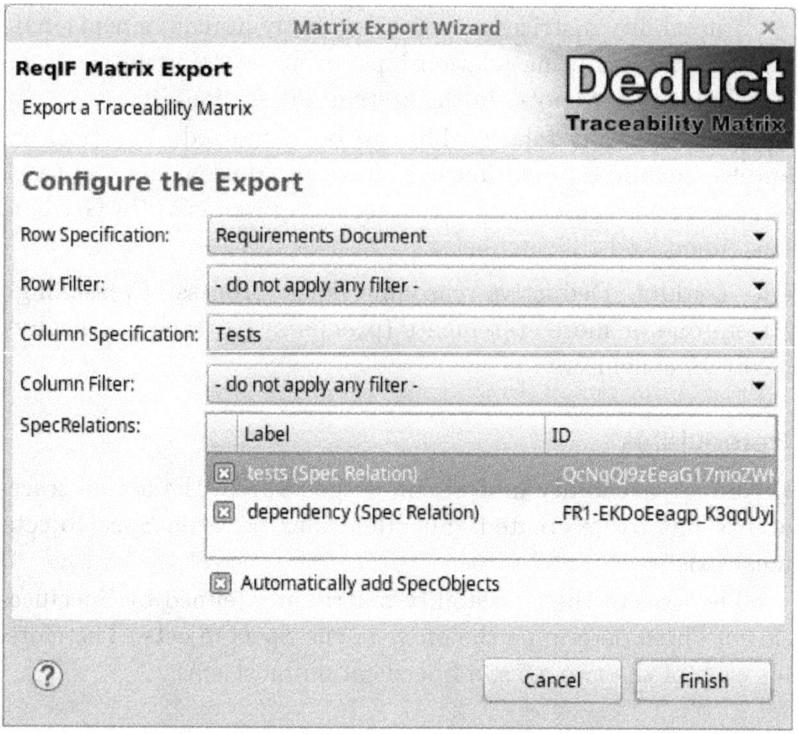

Figure 5.14: The dialog for configuring the traceability matrix

Irrespective on how Deduct was launched, the wizard shown in Figure 5.14 is opened. The configuration works as follows:

Row Specification. The dropdown lists all Specifications in the file. The chosen Specification will be used for determining the elements that appear on the rows, as well as their order. The hierarchy of the Specification will be collapsed. In other words: The order of the SpecObjects is the same as in the SPECIFICATION EDITOR, but the hierarchy will not be visible any more.

Row Filter. The dropdown will list all configured filters (see Section 7.7.2. A chosen filter will be applied to the *Row Specification* elements and may reduce the list.

Column Specification. Corresponding to *Row Specification* for columns.

Column Filter. Corresponding to *Row Filter* for columns.

SpecRelations. The list shows all *SpecRelationTypes* that exist

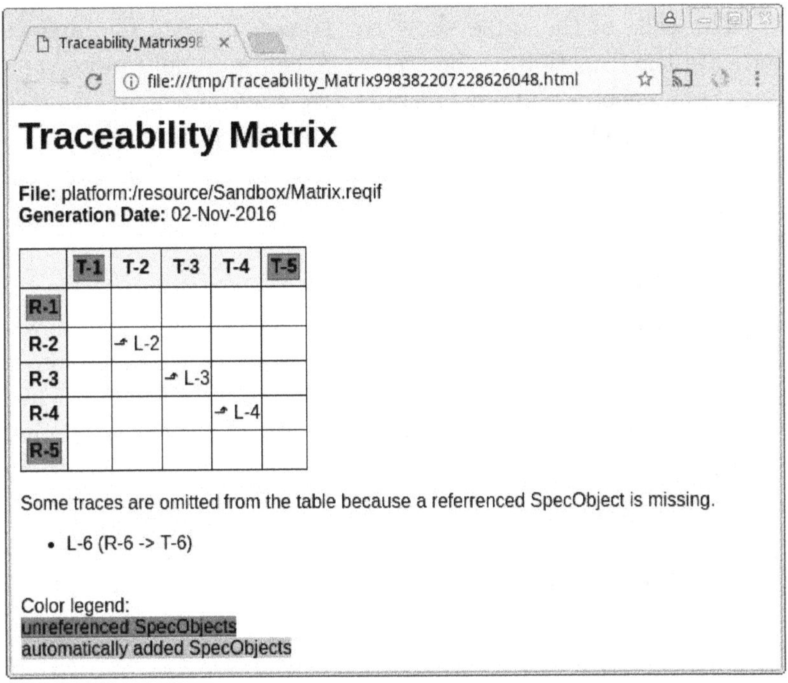

Traceability Matrix

File: platform:/resource/Sandbox/Matrix.reqif
Generation Date: 02-Nov-2016

	T-1	T-2	T-3	T-4	T-5
R-1					
R-2		↰ L-2			
R-3			↰ L-3		
R-4				↰ L-4	
R-5					

Some traces are omitted from the table because a referrenced SpecObject is missing.

- L-6 (R-6 -> T-6)

Color legend:
unreferenced SpecObjects
automatically added SpecObjects

Figure 5.15: A generated traceability matrix.

in the model. The chosen ones will be used to fill the traceability matrix.

Automatically add SpecObjects. There is the possibility that SpecRelations require SpecObjects that are not found on the axes – either due to a filter, or because they are not referenced from the selected Specifications. Checking this flag will add those SpecObject to the end of the respective axis. If the flag is unchecked, a list of missing SpecRelations will be included in the output.

> (i) The labels for Rows, Columns and SpecRelations are taken from the file's *Label configuration* via STUDIO | GENERAL CONFIGURATION | LABEL CONFIGURATION.

5.4.3 Interpreting the Output

The resulting traceability matrix is generated as HTML and opened in the system's web browser, as shown in Figure 5.15. The title is taken from the ReqIF's title attribute.

The cells of the table show the traces, if any. The arrows indicate the direction of the traces. A cell may hold more then one trace, each in one row, with its arrow and label.

Some SpecObjects may be highlighted in red (e.g. R-1). This indicated that there is no trace from or to the given element. This can help finding gaps in the traceability.

5.4.4 CSV Export

The page with the generated HTML also contains a link to download the matrix as a CSV file. CSV can easily be imported into a spreadsheet application like *Microsoft Excel* or *LibreOffice Calc*.

The exported file only contains the matrix, not the additional information like file name, missing links, etc. This makes it easy to automatically process the resulting file.

> (i) There are many variations to CSV. The CSV export from this tool conforms to RFC4180.

5.4.5 Handling Missing SpecObjects

In Figure 5.15, below the table is a "missing links" list. for the matrix shown, the flag AUTOMATICALLY ADD SPECOBJECTS was unchecked. However, the SpecRelation L-6 could not be shown in the table. It is listed here instead.

Alternatively, the flag could have been checked. In that case, the two SpecObjects R-6 and T-6 would be added automatically. The result is shown in Figure 5.16. SpecObjects that had to be added are highlighted in orange.

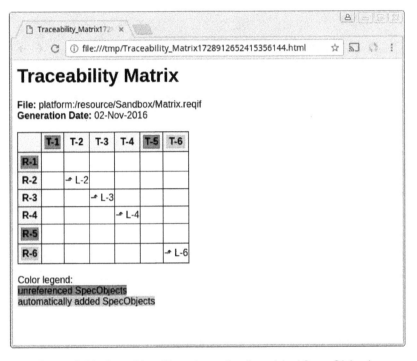

Figure 5.16: A matrix with automatically added SpecObjects.

6. Customization

ReqIF Studio is a useful tool, "as is," but, to really get the most out of it, you can customize it heavily by installing new plug-ins from the Eclipse ecosystem.

You can visit the Eclipse Website[1] to find out about the available plug-ins and features. It is a daunting offering. Therefore, in the following, we describe the more useful offerings, and how to install them.

6.1 Team Work and Version Control

ReqIF Studio does not come with versioning built in. But in practice, you need it for two reasons: First, you want to be able to go back in time, for instance, if you want to restore a requirement. Second, you need versioning to operate in a team setting, so that you know who made which change.

▶ **Repository.** The repository is the place where your versioned data is stored. You can think of it as a database. Tools like Subversion have a single repository, while with distributed systems like git, each user has their own repository (which can be synchronized with a central repository).

---

[1]http://eclipse.org

▶ **Commit.** Committing is the process of sending your changes since the last commit to the repository. When going back in history later on, you can only see the difference between two commits, but not more granular changes.

There are a number of well-supported versioning systems available as Eclipse plug-ins. The most popular ones are git and Subversion. These were initially designed for managing source code, but they work fine for models, if properly configured.

ⓘ Professional requirements engineering tools typically require a server to operate. By working with a versioning system, you need a server as well. But this server can also reside on the computer you are working with. Alternatively or complementary, you can use the Axiom component (Chapter 5.1) to asynchronously collaborate with partners, without a server.

6.1.1 Configuring ReqIF Studio for Team Work

In the following, we will describe various repository systems. But irrespective to which one you use, there are a few things that you should configure in ReqIF Studio. Specifically, disable model ID generation.] By default, and as required by the standard, different ReqIF files must have different IDs. This is the standard behavior of ReqIF Studio, which generates a new ID upon each save. But this will guarantee conflicts in a team environment. Therefore, this can be disabled via WINDOW | PREFERENCES | REQIF | GENERATE A NEW REQIF ID ON SAVE.

ⓘ Team work support is high on the tool's roadmap. Please check roadmap and progress at ReqIF.academy (https://reqif.academy).

6.1.2 Repository Technologies

Versioning systems broadly fall into two categories, distributed and non-distributed. In a distributed system, each user has their own repository (with a complete history). Typically there is a "master" repository that everybody synchronizes with. This does not differ technically, it's special status is just a designation.

Centralized (non-distributed) repositories have a central repository server. No synchronization is necessary, but commits are only possible if the central server is reachable. Centralized repositories allow "locking" of individual files, ensuring that only one person works on them at a time. This prevents conflicts (which can be bad, especially on binary files), but inhibits scalability.

The following list describes the more popular repository technologies

Subversion (centralized) is a popular version control system that requires connection with the server when "committing" files. It is not very good in merging conflicts or branches.

git (distributed) is a distributed version control system. Using a server is optional, but recommended for team work. Even with a server, it allows you to commit changes without connecting to it. Locking is not supported. It has really good merge support. It is newer and has explicitly made an attempt to make things better than other established tools.

Mercurial (distributed) is another distributed system that is very similar to git.

CVS (centralized) is an older repository system. It's use for new projects is discouraged, as the previously mentioned tools are significantly better.

6.1.3 git

In the following, we describe how you install, configure and work with a git repository for versioning and team support.

> ⓘ The following describes how to work with a local repository. If you need a test **server** environment to play around with git, we recommend to sign up for a free gitHub account[2]. gitHub is a free online platform that provides personal git repositories. More about this in Section 6.1.4.

Installation

. You need the following update site:

- The installation process is described in Section 7.2.4
- Use this update site: http://download.eclipse.org/egit/updates
- Install ECLIPSE GIT TEAM PROVIDER

---

[2]http://github.org

Configuration

To configure your project with a repository (git or otherwise), follow these steps:

- Start with an existing project in your workspace (a top-level folder in the Project Explorer).
- Right-click on the project you want to add to the repository and select TEAM | SHARE PROJECT....
- In the case of git, you will see a dialog that allows you to configure the repository.
- Click on CREATE... to select a folder where your local repository files will be stored.
- Click FINISH.

Upon completion, the project icon will be decorated with information regarding the repository state.

Adding and Committing Files

To actually commit your project and project files to the repository, you have to perform these steps:

- Add the files that should be submitted to the index via right-click and TEAM | ADD TO INDEX. Files will be added recursively. Upon completion, the decoration of the files will change to reflect the new state.
- You can ignore files by right-clicking and selecting TEAM | IGNORE.
- Commit files via right-click and selecting TEAM | COMMIT.... You can provide a commit message.
- Hit COMMIT to commit to the repository. The COMMIT AND PUSH option also pushes the changes to a central server (if configured) and is described in Section 6.1.4.

▶ **Index (git).** The git index is a place where information that is to be committed is stored. This allows you to only commit some parts of your local modifications.

History and Comparing

The commit history can be accessed via TEAM | SHOW IN HISTORY. The history view will be opened, if it is not open yet and shown in Figure 6.1.

The history provides a number of actions, which can be accessed via the toolbar and context menu. The top pane shows the history of the repository, while the lower pane shows details of

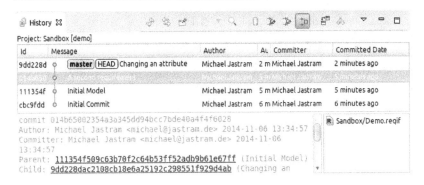

Figure 6.1: The history allow the inspection of past versions of the project files.

the selected element. You can apply the history view on a single file or the project as a whole.

> For detailed information, please consult the EGit Eclipse Handbook[3].

The more interesting actions are:

- Right-click on a revision and select COMPARE WITH WORKSPACE to see the differences.
- Select **two revisions**, right-click and select COMPARE WITH EACH OTHER to see the differences between them.
- Right-click on a revision and select CHECKOUT to replace the workspace version with the selected one.

> ReqIF Studio ships with an extension to the generic compare tool, which makes it ReqIF specific. This is described in Section 6.2.

6.1.4 Using a Repository Server

If you want to collaborate with other team members, you need a shared repository. In the previous example, we used a local folder on your hard drive. In the real world, there would be a dedicated server holding the shared repository.

---

[3]http://help.eclipse.org/luna/topic/org.eclipse.egit.doc/help/EGit/ User_Guide/User-Guide.html?cp=1

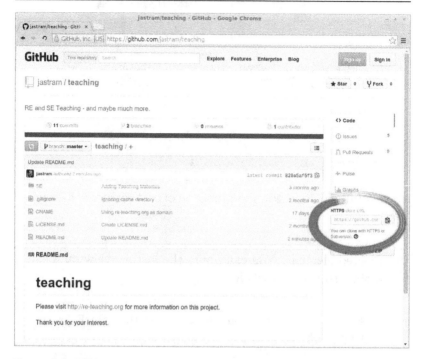

Figure 6.2: gitHub makes it easy to play with git repositories. The clone URL is shown on the right.

A quick way that is particularly useful for testing is to use gitHub[4], which allows the creation of free repositories on a server within a few minutes. Keep in mind that free repositories are always public. If you need a private repository, we recommend that you set up your own server. You can also pay a service provider for a private repository, including gitHub.

Before you can start, you need a git repository URL. If you created a repository on gitHub, the main repository page will show you the repository URL on the right hand side (see Figure 6.2).

The main difference to the previous workflow is that synchronization with the server has to be triggered explicitly. Specifically:

Pull. Retrieves the latest version from the server and merges it into the local repository. This can result in a merge conflict that has to be resolved manually.

Push. Sends the latest version from the local repository to the server. A push can fail if the server repository has changed

---

[4]http://github.org

since the last pull.

ⓘ There are other repository technologies besides git, as
   described in Section 6.1.2, but the general workflow is
   always similar.

6.1.5 Baselines

Baselines are special versions, or configurations of information.
The concept of baselines can be realized in version control systems
by using "tags" or "labels".

6.2 Comparing Models (free)

ReqIF Studio provides an extension to the generic compare tool
from Eclipse. This is described in the Formal Mind Blog[5].

ⓘ The compare can be configured in the Preferences WIN-
   DOW | PREFERENCES. Make sure that in EMF COMPARE
   | ENGINES, the ReqIF match engine is activated. Also, in
   PROR | REQIF DIFF, a list of attributes to be ignored
   can be configured.

The tool is currently rather basic. Formal Mind offers a
commercial compare tool that comes bundled with some of our
Components, like Axiom.

6.3 Comparing Models with Binom (commercial)

Work on requirements rarely happens in isolation, as has already
been pointed out in Section 6.1. And an important part of team
work is comparing requirements, and sometimes merging conflicts.
    The built-in compare facility is rather limited. If you need a
more sophisticated, scalable compare functionality, then please
consider getting Binom, which is described in Chapter 5.2.

ⓘ Highlights of the commercial compare with Binom include
   the visualization of document structures, comparing of
   attributes side by side, filtering, and much more. Learn
   more in Chapter 5.2.

---

[5]http://formalmind.com/en/blog/comparing-reqif-files-pror-essentials-
diff

ReqIF Studio Installation
Eclipse
ReqIF Studio User Interface
Configuration and Preferences
Access Control
Import and Export
Searching and Filtering

7. Reference

This chapter will give you concise information regarding all aspects of ReqIF Studio.

7.1 ReqIF Studio Installation

ReqIF Studio is a desktop application based on Eclipse for systems engineering in general, and requirements engineering in particular. It can be installed standalone, or as part of an existing Eclipse installation.

7.1.1 Installation as Standalone Product

ReqIF Studio can be downloaded from the ReqIF Academy[1]. It can then be installed like a regular Eclipse product, as described in Section 7.2.2.

7.1.2 Installation in Eclipse 3

ReqIF Studio can be installed into an existing Eclipse installation. It works with Eclipse 3.8 or better. For Eclipse 4, see Section 7.1.3.

Installation is done via update sites. This is described in detail in Section 7.2.4. Essentially, you need to start Eclipse,

---

[1]https://reqif.academy

select HELP | INSTALL NEW SOFTWARE... and configure the
installation wizard with the provided information.

ⓘ If you need rich text (XHTML) support, then you first
need to install e(fx)clipse. Otherwise continue with the
Essentials installation below. To install e(fx)clipse:
- Enter the following URL: http://download.eclipse.
org/efxclipse/runtime-released/0.9.0/site.
- Select FX RUNTIME, proceed with the installation
and restart.

ⓘ If you need EMF Compare (for visual comparing) support,
then you first need to install it. Note that EMF Compare
is already part of some Eclipse installations, in that case
you can skip this step as well.

If you do not need EMF Compare, continue with the
Essentials installation below. To install EMF Compare:
- Enter the following URL: http://download.eclipse.
org/modeling/emf/compare/updates/releases.
- Select EMF COMPARE | EMF COMPARE RCP UI
(and nothing else!), proceed with the installation
and restart.

To install Essentials, again start the installation wizard and:
- Enter the following URL: http://update.formalmind.com/
essentials.
- Select ESSENTIALS. You can either select individual components or all of them.
- But if you decide not to install the above features, you need
to remove the corresponding elements from the category,
otherwise the dependencies will not be fulfilled.

Upon completion, ReqIF Studio will be part of your Eclipse
installation.

7.1.3   Installation in Eclipse 4

Installing ReqIF Studio into an existing Eclipse 4 installation
works similar to installing it into Eclipse 3. The main difference
is that the rich text (XHTML) feature requires a different update
site.

To use the rich text feature (XHTML), please install e(fx)clipse from this update site: http://download.eclipse.org/efxclipse/runtime-released/1.1.0/site

7.2 Eclipse

ReqIF Studio is an extension of the generic Eclipse Platform. The following is concerned with Eclipse in general.

 Please consult the Eclipse platform overview[2] for further information.

7.2.1 Prerequisites

Eclipse is a Java-based application. You need a Java Runtime Environment (JRE) on your computer in order to run ReqIF Studio.

ReqIF Studio requires JRE 1.6 or better. However, some of the features from Essentials require JRE 1.7 or better. Further, we recommend the version from Oracle, and not OpenJDK.

 You can download Java at java.com[3].

7.2.2 Installation

This chapter explores the installation of *Eclipse Products*, i.e. software that you can download and run on your computer. This is in contrast to *features* or *plugins*, which can be added to an existing product.

When working with Eclipse, you have to start with a base installation. However, we recommend using ReqIF Studio[4], but you can start with any Eclipse product.

Once you have identified the product you would like to use, you need to download it, which is typically a .zip file. Create a folder and extract the content of the .zip file into that folder.

---

[2]http://help.eclipse.org/luna/topic/org.eclipse.platform.doc.user/gettingStarted/intro/overview.htm?cp=0_0

[3]https://www.java.com

[4]https://reqif.academy

We recommend to call the folder STUDIO and to store it where your executables are located: On Windows in PROGRAM FILES, on Linux in /BIN. But any location will do.

We recommend to creating a shortcut for launching it.

You launch the product by double-clicking on the launcher in the folder you created. For ReqIF Studio, this is called STUDIO.EXE or STUDIO.

The first time you launch Eclipse, it will ask you for the *Workspace* location, see Section 7.2.5.

7.2.3 Updates

The Eclipse Update Manager regularly checks for new versions and alerts the user if one is found. It can also be started manually via HELP | CHECK FOR UPDATES.

7.2.4 Installing New Features

Before you start installing new features, you typically need to connect with the update site that is hosting the feature to be installed.

> ► **Update Site.** An update site is a machine-readable URL that allows ReqIF Studio to install new functionality. Note that visiting the update site with a web browser rarely produces anything meaningful.

To install a new feature, follow these steps:

- Open the installation dialog via HELP | INSTALL NEW SOFTWARE....
- In the WORK WITH: dropbox, either paste the Update Site URL, or select it from the drop down, if you have used it before. Note that some popular update site URLs may already be preinstalled.
- Upon selecting an update site, you will see a list of components available from that update site. Note the checkboxes below that may result in some entries being hidden. In particular, some update sites do not categorize. Unchecking GROUP ITEMS BY CATEGORY may unveil hidden entries.
- Click NEXT >. If all dependencies can be resolved, details about the installation are shown. Otherwise you have to

troubleshoot dependencies (an unthankful job!).

- Click NEXT >, review and accept the license.
- Click FINISH. If the component has not been digitally signed, you will receive a warning, which you can typically ignore.
- It is recommended to restart after the installation.

> (i) **Signatures on Content.** In this day and age, security is obviously very important, particularly for content downloaded from the Internet. But note that signing is not enough: content must be signed with a trusted, non-expired signature.
>
> Eclipse content should be signed by eclipse.org. Especially small project release plug-ins that are not signed, reasoning that to a user, a self-signed signature is as good (or bad) as a missing signature.
>
> Ultimately, you need to decide for yourself whether you are willing to run unsigned and/or untrusted content.

7.2.5 Workspaces

The workspace is a folder on your computer, where all information related to ReqIF Studio is stored. This includes all your ReqIF files, organized into projects, as well as various meta data.

> (i) Read more about the The Workbench[5] in the Eclipse documentation.
>
> Also, it is possible to have more than one workspace, and to switch between them. This feature can be useful for advanced users.

7.2.6 Committer License Agreement (CLA)

The Committer License Agreement (CLA) needs to be signed by contributors to Eclipse projects. It essentially states that you hold all rights to your contribution and that you allow Eclipse to use them under the Eclipse Public License.

7.3 ReqIF Studio User Interface

Figure 7.1 shows the user interface of ReqIF Studio.

---

[5]http://help.eclipse.org/luna/topic/org.eclipse.platform.doc.user/ gettingStarted/qs-02a.htm?cp=0_1_0_0

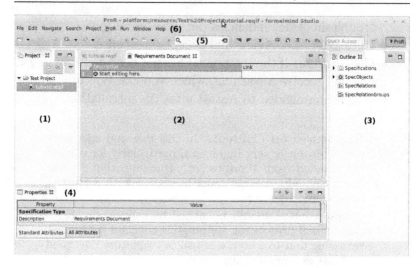

Figure 7.1: The ReqIF Studio user interface

(1)

The PROJECT EXPLORER shows a hierarchical listing of the project and the associated models.

(2)

The editor area shows two kinds of editors. First, each ReqIF file has a REQIF EDITOR that shows basic information about the mode. In addition, SPECIFICATION EDITORS can be opened for each Specification.

(3)

The OUTLINE VIEW has four folders that show the content of the selected model:

Specifications shows the Specifications in the ReqIF model. You can expand the tree to expose the hierarchy of SpecObjects in each Specification.

SpecObjects shows all SpecObjects in the ReqIF model as a flat list. Keep in mind that SpecObjects in Specifications are references. In contrast, this folder shows all SpecObjects created for the ReqIF model, whether or not they are referenced.

SpecRelations shows all SpecRelations in the ReqIF as a flat list.

SpecRelationsGroups represents an optional mechanism for

Figure 7.2: Views.

grouping SpecRelations between two specific specifications.

(4)

The properties of a selected Element are shown in the PROPER-
TIES VIEW. It has two tabs, one for STANDARD ATTRIBUTES and
one for ALL ATTRIBUTES.

(5)

Above the main working windows is the tool bar, which may
change according to which editor is active.

(6)

The menu bar provides access to all Eclipse and ReqIF Studio
features.

7.3.1 Editors and Views

The Eclipse user interface consists of *Views* and *Editors*. Views
change their content according to the current selection and are
not savable. Editors are typically associated with a resource (e.g.
a file) and can be saved. The editors' selection can determine
what is shown in the Views. For instance, the PROPERTIES
VIEW typically shows details about the element selected in the
SPECIFICATION EDITOR.

You can browse through the available Views and open them
via WINDOW | SHOW VIEWS..., resulting in a menu similar to
the one shown in Figure 7.2.

Figure 7.3: ReqIF Editor

Upon opening a ReqIF model, the editor opens providing an overview of the model. In essence what you are seeing is the Eclipse Workbench, with several modifications. Here you will find a quick overview of each component. A more detailed description of the Workbench can be found in Eclipse's Workbench User Guide[6].

> (i) There may be more than one editor for a given file type. To pick a specific one, right-click the file and select OPEN WITH..., which will give you the list of installed editors. In particular, the REQIF STUDIO MAIN EDITOR from Formal Mind is more powerful than the stock editor (see Section 7.3.4).

A model contains any number of Specifications, and the details of each Specification can be inspected individually. The windows in which all relevant information appears are called *views*. At your disposal are many views with productivity, debugging, help and team resources. We will be focusing only on the views relevant to ReqIF Studio.

7.3.2   ReqIF Editor

The REQIF EDITOR is the first editor that opens when opening a ReqIF file. It is shown in Figure 7.3.

---

[6]http://help.eclipse.org/lunaorg.eclipse.platform.doc.user/reference/ref-43.htm

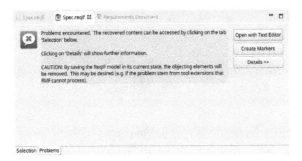

Figure 7.4: ReqIF Editor with an active error tab

The REQIF EDITOR lists all Specifications, which can be opened by double-clicking.

(i) If only one Specification is contained in the ReqIF file, it is opened automatically in a SPECIFICATION EDITOR.

Further, there are a few sections that are collapsed by default:

RMF – Getting Started. This section contains some basic information for new users.

Document Properties. This section show the embedded metadata. Some of it can be edited, some elements are read-only, as they are set by the tool.

7.3.3 Errors in ReqIF Editor

If a ReqIF file is invalid, then ReqIF Studio makes an attempt to recover. If this succeeds, then the REQIF EDITOR will show two tabs, as shown in Figure 7.4.

On the bottom, the editor now has two tabs, labeled SELECTION and PROBLEMS. The PROBLEMS tab has three options:

Open with Text Editor. This button will open the raw XML in a text editor. It is recommended to press CREATE MARKERS first.

Create Markers. This button will create error markers. This helps to pinpoint the problematic XML in the text editor.

Details. This will open an area showing the error tree. This information will also be shown in the PROBLEM VIEW.

The SELECTION tab shows the recovered ReqIF. Depending on the reason for the error condition, most or even all of the ReqIF is still there.

Saving the file will remove all problematic elements.

(i) A problematic ReqIF file can be fixed by simply by saving
the ReqIF file again. It is recommended to inspect hte
recovered ReqIF first, and to make a backup.

7.3.4 Formal Mind Specification Editor

Formal Mind provides their own, improved editor. If you are
using ReqIF Studio, then the new editor should be the default.
You can recognize it by its icon ▣.

(!) Once you explicitly uses an editor for a file, this choice
is overwritten for that file. You can recognize the editor
you use by its icon.

Switching between Editors

If the Formal Mind editor is installed, it is the default when
opening a file. It is possible to explicitly select an editor via
RIGHT-CLICK | OPEN WITH....

Viewing large content

The standard editor truncates content, as large rows don't scroll
properly. The Formal Mind editor does the same, but hovering
over a truncated cell exposes it's content in an overlay.

The overlay can be dismissed by pressing ESC or simply by
moving the mouse away. Within the overlay, the cursor keys and
PGUP/PGDOWN allow scrolling.

Rearranging Columns

The new editor allows columns to be rearranged by drag and drop.
The column being dragged is inserted to the left of the column it
is dropped on.

7.3.5 Working with Model Elements

The ReqIF Studio user interface allows you to manipulate all aspects of the the ReqIF data model – the most important functions
were demonstrated in the Tutorial (see Chapter 3). However,
the actual ReqIF data model does not have a good a very useful
structure. Therefore, the structure presented throught the user
interface differs from the actual ReqIF data model.

For most operations, this does not really matter. But there are a few aspects that you need to look out for, specifically deleting and copying.

Deleting SpecObjects

Most elements can just be deleted and will be gone. But SpecObjects are usually edited in the Specification Editor (Section 7.3.4). However, there is another construct between Specification and SpecObject, the Spec Hiearchy. This means that in ReqIF Studio, a SpecObject can be referenced multiple times.

Therefore, when deleting a SpecObject from the Specification Editor, it is not obvious whether only the SpecHirarchy is deleted, or both SpecHirarchy and SpecObject.

To solve this dilemma, ReqIF Studio will delete only the SpecHierarchy, if there is more than one reference to the connected SpecObject. If the last reference to a SpecObject is deleted, ReqIF Studio will show a dialog, informing the user user that the connected SpecObject will be deleted as well. The user has the option to cancel.

The user has the option to change this behavior in the preferences. If changed, deleting the last reference to a SpecObject will result in "dead objects" – SpecObjects that are not references from any Specification.

   (i)   Dead SpecObjects can still be accessed via the Outline of the main editor (Section 7.3.1.

Pasting SpecObjects

When copying a SpecObject via the Specification Editor, a reference to the original SpecObject is created. In other words, a new SpecHierarchy is created which points to the original SpecObject.

   (!)   If the user does not understand the concept of multiple references to a SpecObject, it is possible to accidentally change a SpecObject when it is not intended.

7.3.6 RMF Specification Editor

The Specification Editor shows the SpecObjects of a Specification, arranged in a grid view. The hierarchy is shown via the indent

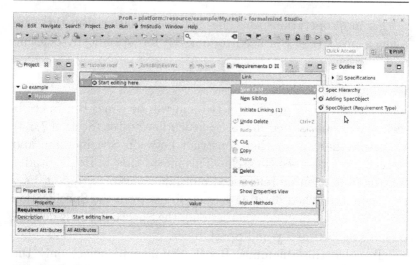

Figure 7.5: Specification Editor with the context menu open for creating a new child element

of the first column, as well as through the numbering in the row header.

The columns show the Attributes with the names that match the column names (as shown in the header). The columns can be resized by dragging. Other operations, in particular reordering, adding and deleting columns are done via the COLUMN DIALOG, accessible via STUDIO | COLUMN CONFIGURATION or the toolbar ▦.

The leftmost column shows the hierarchy and carries an icon. The icon indicates whether it is a lone SpecHierarchy ○ or a SpecObject ⊕.

> (i) Would you like to rearrange the columns?
> In ReqIF Studio, you can simply drag the columns by grabbing them by their headers.
> In Eclipse RMF, this does not work. Instead, use the following approach, which also works with ReqIF Studio: In the top half of the COLUMN CONFIGURATOR ▦ window, a list of the exiting columns appear. Simply drag and drop them into the desired order. The changes appear in real time in the SPECIFICATION EDITOR. Close the window and the changes will be accepted.

Information can be entered either directly into the cell by

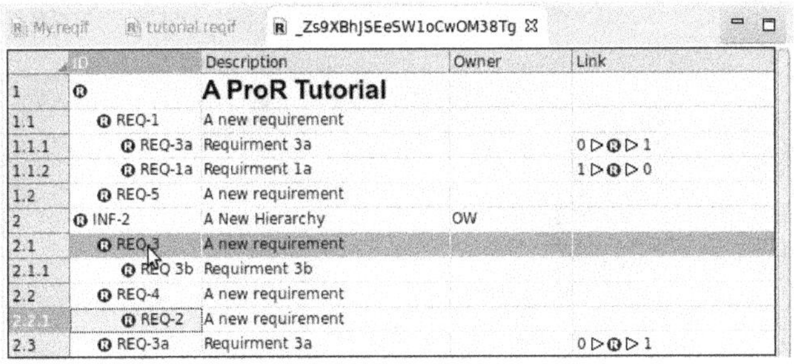

Figure 7.6: Click on a requirement and drag onto target parent.

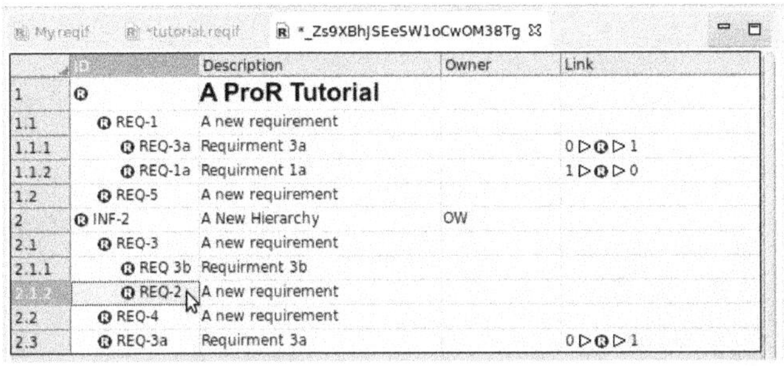

Figure 7.7: Result: The requirement is now a child of the chosen parent.

double-clicking it or via the PROPERTIES VIEW. While the Specification Editor only allows the editing of those attributes for which a column exists, the PROPERTIES VIEW will always show all attributes.

The SpecObjects can be reordered via drag and drop. To move an existing SpecObject into the position of parent or child of another existing SpecObject, simply drag the child directly *onto the target SpecObject*, as shown in Figure 7.6. The result is shown in Figure 7.7.

Alternatively, as you drag the SpecObject *onto the line below or above* the level you would like to move it to, it will become a sibling rather than a child of the SpecObject. This is shown in Figure 7.8, with the resulting ordering shown in Figure 7.9.

To duplicate a SpecObject, simply copy and paste it into the required position. The copying, cutting and pasting functions are accessible through the traditional dropdown menu, by right-clicking on a desired cell or the corresponding keyboard shortcut.

By right clicking on any cell, you have a few options at your

	ID	Description	Owner	Link
1	⊙	**A ProR Tutorial**		
1.1	⊙ REQ-1	A new requirement		
1.1.1	⊙ REQ-3a	Requirement 3a		0 ▷⊙▷ 1
1.1.2	⊙ REQ-1a	Requirment 1a		1 ▷⊙▷ 0
1.2	⊙ REQ-5	A new requirement		
2	⊙ INF-2	A New Hierarchy	OW	
2.1	⊙ REQ-3	A new requirement		
2.1.1	⊙ REQ 3b	Requirment 3b		
2.1.2	⊙ REQ-2	A new requirement		
2.2	⊙ REQ-4	A new requirement		
2.3	⊙ REQ-3a	Requirment 3a		0 ▷⊙▷ 1

Figure 7.8: Click on a requirement and drag onto the line (bolded) below or above target sibling.

	ID	Description	Owner	Link
1	⊙	**A ProR Tutorial**		
1.1	⊙ REQ-1	A new requirement		
1.1.1	⊙ REQ-3a	Requirment 3a		0 ▷⊙▷ 1
1.2	⊙ REQ-5	A new requirement		
	⊙ REQ-1a	Requirment 1a		1 ▷⊙▷ 0
3	⊙ INF-2	A New Hierarchy	OW	
3.1	⊙ REQ-3	A new requirement		
3.1.1	⊙ REQ 3b	Requirment 3b		
3.1.2	⊙ REQ-2	A new requirement		
3.2	⊙ REQ-4	A new requirement		
3.3	⊙ REQ-3a	Requirment 3a		0 ▷⊙▷ 1

Figure 7.9: Result: The requirement is now a sibling of the chosen requirement.

disposal. Outside of the usual UNDO, CUT, COPY, PASTE and DELETE, commands, the following are also available:

New Child. A new SpecObject will be created as a child element.

New Sibling. A new SpecObject will be created as a sibling element.

Initiate Linking. This is the option to create a link between requirements. Once a link is initiated and then by right clicking a target selection, the options to complete the links either to or from a selection will appear. By default, the links are illustrated in the LINK column to the right.

Show Properties View. Opens the PROPERTIES VIEW, where the selected element can be inspected and edited.

7.3.7 Project Explorer View

The PROJECT EXPLORER VIEW is by default on the left side of the main window. Here you can inspect files and models associated with any project. If for some reason the Project Explorer View does not appear, Navigate to WINDOW | SHOW VIEW | OTHER | PROJECT EXPLORER VIEW.

In the main area of this viewer is a hierarchical listing of the project and it's components. Use the black arrow to the left to collapse or display the project's contents. Below the view's title and to the right are the options to collapse the project folder and link the project with the editor. To the right of these options is another dropdown menu.

This view is covered in more detail by the Eclipse documentation[7].

7.3.8 ReqIF Validation

ReqIF is spreading, and partners start handing .reqif and .reqifz files back and forth. But chances are that the first import of such a file will fail. What is the problem? Consequent, the free ReqIF-Validator may provide the answer.

The validation results are shown in the Eclipse Problem View. In addition, it is possible to open the ReqIF file in question in a text editor and to generate error markers, as shown in Figure 7.10.

> (i) In addition to the validator that is built into the tool, there is also a command line version available, which can be downloaded for free from https://reqif.academy.

You can validate a ReqIF file as follows:
- Right-Click the file to be validated in the Project Explorer (no need to open the file)
- Select VALIDATE | CONSEQUENT REQIF VALIDATION
- A dialog indicates the completion of the validation, which is shown in the Problem View.
- If the Problem View is not visible, open it by hand via WINDOW | SHOW VIEW | OTHER... | GENERAL | PROBLEMS

---

[7]http://help.eclipse.org/luna/topic/org.eclipse.platform.doc.user/reference/ref-27.htm

```
<?xml version="1.0" encoding="UTF-8"?>
<REQ-IF xmlns="http://www.omg.org/spec/ReqIF/20110401/reqif.xs
  <THE-HEADER>
  [D]The required feature 'title' of 'ReqIFHeaderImpl' must be set 3b1-41db-95c4-f7
      <COMMENT>Created by: jastram</COMMENT>
      <CREATION-TIME>2015-03-05T16:29:33.969+01:00</CREATION-TI
      REQ-IF-TOOL-ID>ProR (http://pror       </REQ-IF-TOOL-ID>
```

Figure 7.10: Error Markers generated by Consequent

- To see the error in the file, you must open it in a text editor
  as follows:
  - Right-Click the file in the Project Explorer
  - Select Open With | Text Editor
  - Errors are shown with an icon in the left margin (hover-
    ing over the error reveals the problem) – see screenshot
    below
  - For errors with line numbers, it is possible to double
    click on an error in the Problem View to jump to the
    corresponding position in the Text Editor
- Error markers do not reset automatically. Re-run the validation to update them. You can manually clear error markes
  (e.g. for files that do not exist any more) by right-clicking
  on an element in the Problem View and selecting Delete.

Validation Rules

You can access and individually disable the validation rules via
WINDOW | PREFERENCES | MODEL VALIDATION | CONSTRAINTS.

> (i) A printable version of the validation rules can retrieved
> from the build server at http://hudson.eclipse.org/rmf/
> job/rmf.develop.mars/ws/org.eclipse.rmf.reqif10.constraints/
> plugin.xml

Consequent Acknowledgement

Consequent is part of the open source Eclipse project and was
financed by the ProStep ReqIF Implementor Forum.

7.4 Configuration and Preferences

Both the current model, as well as ReqIF Studio as a whole, can
be configured and customized extensively.

7.4.1 Global Preferences

The application-wide settings of ReqIF Studio are accessed via
WINDOW | PREFERENCES | REQIF. Configuration elements are:

ReqIF. In the top level menu, the warning message for encoun-
tering simplified XHTML can be disabled.

Default Presentations. ReqIF Studio has basic cell editors for
each ReqIF *Datatypes*. But it is possible to install new editors with better or different capabilities. With this setting,
Presentations can be selected to handle certain Datatypes
by default.

> (i) Particularly popular is the free Presentation from Es-
> sentials for handling XHTML. The standard editor from
> RMF converts rich text to plain text. The rich text
> Presentation is preinstalled with ReqIF Studio.

7.4.2 General Configuration

This configuration is accessed either via STUDIO | GENERAL
CONFIGURATION, or via the ⚹ button on the toolbar.

Currently, there is only one configuration element: LABEL
CONFIGURATION.

Label Configuration

The LABEL CONFIGURATION is used to determine what to use for
the text labels of elements in places, where a shorthand is needed.
Examples are elements in the OUTLINE VIEW or the link targets
in the LINK column.

ReqIF Studio will determine the label by looking at the LABEL
CONFIGURATION, which is a list of text strings (see Figure 7.11.
To identify the label of an element, ReqIF Studio will go through
the list, top to bottom. If the element has an attribute with a
matching name, that attribute value is used as the label.

If none is found, then the element's internal ID is displayed.

Figure 7.11 provides an example. For instance, the label
for a SpecObject in the OUTLINE VIEW is found by first looking for an attribute named "ReqIF.ChapterNumber". If one is
found, it is used as the label. If not, ReqIF Studio looks for
"ReqIF.ChapterName", and so on, until one is found. If none is
found, the internal ID is used.

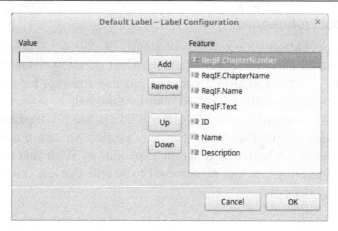

Figure 7.11: The Label Configuration consists of a list of attribute names. To find the label for a SpecElement, the list is scanned from top to bottom to find a matching attribute, which is then used as the label. If none is found, the internal ID is used.

To configure, select LABEL CONFIGURATION in the top pane of the dialog. On the bottom pane, you see the DEFAULT LABEL property. Doubleclick the value (on the right), then click on the ellipses (...) to open the configuration dialog. Under FEATURE, you will see the list of attribute names that will be used for the label, if found.

Use the ADD and REMOVE buttons to add more attribute names to be searched for. The search order can be adjusted with UP and DOWN.

> (i) It is good practice to use the ID Presentation (4.3.1) to generate user-friendly IDs, and to use these as the first match for a label. As IDs are unique, you'll always have a unique identifier that is typically also used for communication.

7.4.3 Datatype Configuration

This configuration is opened via STUDIO | DATATYPE CONFIGURATION...

The dialog shows two folders, one for SpecTypes and one for Datatypes. SpecTypes are created for typing elements that have attributes (SpecObjects, Specifications, SpecRelations). New SpecTypes can be created by right-clicking on the folder and

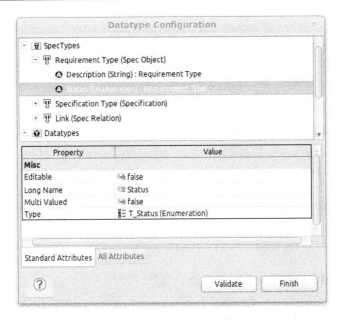

Figure 7.12: Datatype Configuration Dialog

selecting NEW CHILD. Through the same mechanism, attribute definitions can be added to a SpecType. Attribute definitions are typed. Selecting an element shows its properties in the lower pane, where it can be configured.

Attributes must have a name and a Datatype. Some Attributes allow further customization. The Datatype is selected from a dropdown. New Datatypes can be created by right-clicking on the folder DATATYPES and selecting NEW CHILD. Again, selecting a Datatype shows its properties in the lower pane, where it can be configured. A Datatype should have at least the LONG NAME property set.

As an example, consider the Datatype Configuration shown in Figure 7.12. The SpecType for "Requirements Type," which is applicable to SpecObjects, is expanded. The SpecType has two Attributes, "Description" (String) and "Status" (Enumeration). Status is selected, and in the pane below the mandatory values, LONG NAME and TYPE have been set. Further customization of the attribute is possible, e.g. by converting it to a multi-valued Attribute by setting the corresponding flag to TRUE.

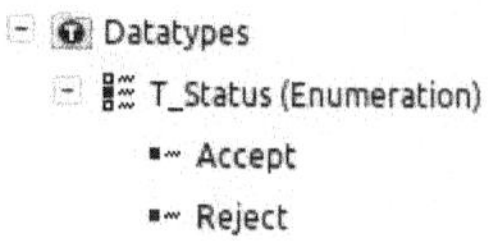

```
⊟  ◙  Datatypes
    ⊟  ▥  T_Status (Enumeration)
        ▪~  Accept
        ▪~  Reject
```

Figure 7.13: Enumerations

Enumeration Datatypes

An Enumeration Datatype must have enumeration values. These are created by right-clicking the Enumeration Datatype and selecting NEW CHILD |ENUM VALUE. You may have to unfold the enum value to select it, so that you can provide it with a LONG NAME. Figure 7.13 shows a correctly configured Enumeration Datatype.

7.4.4 Presentation Configuration

Presentations are software components that extend the functionality of ReqIF Studio. Chapter 4 is dedicated to Presentations.

7.4.5 Column Configuration

This configuration is specific to the Specification Editor.

The Column Configuration Dialog configures the Columns of a Specification. Columns are identified by name. The width of the column can be adjusted directly by dragging the column separator in the table header.

If the SpecObject has an attribute where the name of the attribute matches the name of the column, then that attribute is shown in that column.

7.5 Access Control

The ReqIF standard provides a flag for marking certain elements as read-only. This flag is accessible through the PROPERTIES VIEW by selecting the tab ALL ATTRIBUTES. However, this flag is not honored in the user interface: even if an element is marked as read-only, it is normally writable. We may implement this in the future.

> ⓘ   Access Control is a ReqIF feature designed for data exchange. As ReqIF Studio uses ReqIF as a data model

(and not as an exchange format), access information is only stored, but not used for managing access.

7.6 Import and Export

Importers and Exporters are accessed via FILE | IMPORT... and FILE | EXPORT.... The corresponding dialogs will show generic Importers and Exporters, as well as specific ones. The specific ones are in a folder called REQIF STUDIO (REQIF).

This section also lists Importers and Exporters from third parties. Note that not all third-party Importers and Exporters may be listed here.

7.6.1 Import

The following importers exist:

ReqIFz Import. This standard importer takes ReqIF archive (.reqifz) and imports it as an Eclipse project.

CSV. This standard importer takes comma-separated data and imports it into an existing ReqIF model. It is described further below.

Axiom. This commercial importer supports the selective merging of exchange data with an existing ReqIF model. It is described in detail in Section 5.1.

More information at the ReqIF Academy[8].

CSV Import

The CSV import adds the content from a comma-separated file into an existing specification. Therefore, you first need to create a ReqIF model. Once this is done, the importer is used as follows:

> (!) The importer will create new SpecTypes, Attributes and Datatypes. Your existing types will not be reused! We recommend to clean up the datatypes after the import.

- Initiate the importer via FILE | IMPORT... | REQIF | CSV.
- On the first dialog page, you need to select the source file containing the CSV data. The dialog defaults to comma-separated data, but other separators can be chosen as well.

---

[8]https://reqif.academy

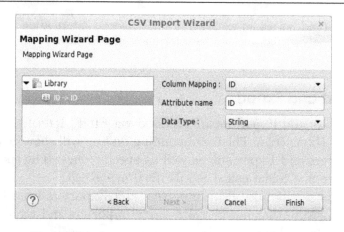

Figure 7.14: A complete mapping for a CSV import

- A checkbox allows to indicated whether the file contains a header row. If it is checked, the first row will be interpreted as the labels for the columns in the file.
- Last, the destination model has to be chosen. After this, the NEXT button is enabled.
- On the next page, the columns have to be mapped. Initially, there is just a single element, LIBRARY.
- Right-click LIBRARY to open the context menu that allows you to add a new mapping. There are four options. They all do the same, but the first three prepopulate the attribute name with a sensible value.
- You need to create a mapping for each column that you would like to import. A mapping consists of three elements:
  Column Mapping. Select the column from the CSV file. The column headings are shown if the checkbox was selected on the previous page, otherwise just the column numbers.
  Attribute Name. The name for the Attribute in the resulting ReqIF model.
  Data Type. The datatype of the resulting attribute. The safest option is STRING, for other datatypes, a conversation attempt is made.
- You do not need to create a mapping for all columns. Figure7.14 shows the importer dialog with one complete mapping.

- Once all mappings are complete, hitting finish will complete the import.

You can read more in the Formal Mind Blog[9].

7.6.2 Export

The following exporters exist:

ReqIFz Export. This standard exporter takes an Eclipse project and produces a ReqIF archive (.reqifz).

Axiom. This commercial exporter supports the selective exporting of exchange data for supplier communication. More information at the ReqIF Academy[10].

HTML. The HTML export is not a "real" export, as it is accessed differently. It produces an HTML view from an open Specification. To use it, you need to have a Specification Editor open. Then select FILE | PRINT....

7.7 Searching and Filtering

ReqIF Studio has three search interfaces. Each has a different focus:

Quicksearch (Section 7.7.1). This interface allows search-as-you-type in the open editor. It is useful for quickly finding the right row in a specification, but just performs a simple text search on all attributes.

ReqIF Search (Section 7.7.2). This interface allow the user-friendly construction of attribute-specific searches within the current model.

Raw Search (Section 7.7.3). This interface is powerful, but requires the queries to be constructed by hand. It allows to fine-tune the search scope, including the search of the whole workspace.

Except the quicksearch, the results are shown in the Eclipse Search Result View[11].

---

[9] http://formalmind.com/blog/new-stuff-new-committer-new-product-new-importer-new-release

[10] https://reqif.academy

[11] http://help.eclipse.org/luna/topic/org.eclipse.platform.doc.user/gettingStarted/qs-36b.htm

7.7.1 Quicksearch

This feature allows you to search-as-you-type within the open Specification. The search box is embedded in the toolbar and only visible if a Specification Editor is open.

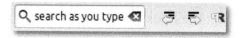

You can just begin typing in the box. With every keystroke, the view will update and collapse those rows that do not match. All attributes are searched.

7.7.2 ReqIF Search

Searching is initiated via SEARCH | SEARCH... | REQIF SEARCH, or via the search icon 🔍 on the toolbar. This will present you the wizard shown in Figure 7.15.

> ⓘ The search dialog shows several tabs on the top. This handbook will cover ReqIF Search and ReqIF Search (Raw)—our ReqIF search tools.
>
> Depending on your Eclipse configuration, other search option may be shown and may still be useful. For instance, the File Search[12] is useful for searching within all files, including .reqif files.

Search Criteria

The ReqIF Search conditions consist of *search criteria*, that are added by clicking on ADD NEW. This creates a new criteria panel. An arbitrary number of criteria can be defined. Criteria can be removed by clicking on × on the left side of the panel, or by clicking CLEAR to remove all.

The radio button on top allows to either MATCH ALL or MATCH ANY of the criteria.

Each criteria consists of three parts, *attribute*, *operator* and *value*. One such criteria is shown in Figure 7.15, with the attribute dropdown open.

---

[12]http://help.eclipse.org/luna/topic/org.eclipse.platform.doc.user/reference/ref-45.htm

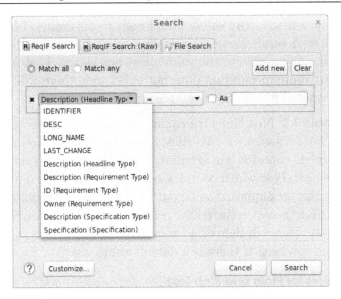

Figure 7.15: ReqIF Search function with attribute dropdown menu

Attribute. Choose an attribute (datatype) from the list. The first four (IDENTIFIER, DESC, LONG_NAME, and LAST_CHANGE) are ReqIF-internal attributes and are rarely of interest to normal users (see Section 2.3.3). The others attributes are taken directly from the document. The more attributes you create, the longer the list will grow. After you have chosen an attribute from the list, the rest of your choices (which are determined by the datatype of the attribute) are displayed.

Operator. The operator dropdown is specific to the selected attribute and is described for each type below.

Value. The value or values are specific to the operator and are also described below.

Operators for All Types

The following operators are available for all attributes, no matter what their type:

Equals (=). For a match, the value must match *exactly* as provided. This implies that the attribute has actually been *set*. For instance, an empty string matches an empty string. But it does not match if the value has not been set (i.e. if it is *null*, in technical terms).

Set. For a match, the value must be set to any value. **Note:** A *default value* does not represent a match.

Not set. For a match, the value must not be set. **Note:** If the attribute in question does not exist, then there will not be a match either. See example below.

▪ **Example 7.1 Not Set Operator.** Assume you receive a ReqIF model for review, with two SpecTypes, one called *Information Type* which contains an attribute *Description* and one called *Requirement Type* which contains two attributes, *Description* and *Status*. You are supposed to fill out the status for all requirements.

To find those that are still missing, you search for STATUS NOT SET. This will deliver all requirements for which no status has been set, even if there is a default value. ▪

Operators for Plain and Rich Text

All text searches can be made case-sensitive by checking the corresponding checkbox AA.

The following operators are available for **plain text** attributes:

Not equals (≠). For a match, the value must not *exactly* as provided. If the attribute is not set, this constitutes a match.

The following operators are available for **plain text and rich text** (XHTML) attributes.

Contains. For a match, the value must be a substring of the attribute.

Contains not. For a match, the value must not be a substring of the attribute. If the attribute is not set, this constitutes a match.

Regexp. The provided value will be interpreted as a regular expression[13]. Search will take place across line breaks.

> ⓘ When searching rich text (XHTML), the invisible formatting will be included in the search, except for the *regexp (plain)* operator described below.
>
> Search will take place across line breaks. But this is only relevant for Regexp search, where linebreaks can be matched explicitly (\ N) or as part of whitespace (\ S).

---

[13]http://help.eclipse.org/luna/topic/org.eclipse.platform.doc.isv/guide/ st_text_types.htm?cp=2_0_3_9_1#regex

The following operators are available for **rich text** (XHTML) attributes.

Regexp (plain). The provided value will be interpreted as a regular expression[14]. Search will take place against a version of the attribute value where the tags have been stripped out and been replaced by whitespace.

■ **Example 7.2 Searching XHTML.** As XHTML contains invisible formatting tags, this should be taken into account when searching. For instance, the search CONTAINS FORMALMIND.COM will find direct textual references to the domain, as well as hyperlinks. e.g. `<a href="http://formalmind.com">click</a>`. ■

Operators for Numbers (Integer and Real)

The interfaces for integer attributes and real attributes are identical, but the text boxes will only accept numbers of the appropriate type.

Not equal ($\neq$). The provided value is not equal to the given number. This operator matches if the attribute has no value set.

Between. A match exists if the attribute value is between the given numbers, **including them**.

Greater than ($>$). A match exists if the attribute value is greater than the value, **excluding it**.

Less than ($<$). A match exists if the attribute value is less than the value, **excluding it**.

Operators for Dates

The granularity of the date criteria are one day, while ReqIF Studio date stamps also include the time and have timezones.

Timezones. Dates in ReqIF Studio have timezones. The dates entered in the search interface assume the local time zone. This can have implications if the values in the ReqIF model have been created by a user in a different time zone. For example, consider a date has been written on "Tuesday 23:00" in the time zone of User 1. But for User 2, it is already "Wednesday 01:00". If User 1 would

---

[14]http://help.eclipse.org/luna/topic/org.eclipse.platform.doc.isv/guide/ st_text_types.htm?cp=2_0_3_9_1#regex

search for "Tuesday", there would be a match. But for
User 2, in a different time zone, not.

Equal (=). The day matches, no matter what the time (but
   timezones apply).
Not equal (≠). Any day except the given day, or not set.
Between. A match exists if the attribute value is between the
   given numbers, **including them**.
Before. A match exists if the attribute value is before the date,
   excluding it (i.e. before the time 00:00:00 on that date).
After. A match exists if the attribute value is after the date,
   including it (i.e. after the time 00:00:00 on that date).

Operators for Enumeration

While ReqIF enumerations may be single value or multi value,
this distinction is immaterial for the search functionality.
Not equal (≠). Anything except an identical list will match.
   Note: An empty list matches an unset attribute value.
All. All selected value must also be selected on the attribute (but
   the attribute may have more).
Any. For a match, at least one of the list values must also be set
   on the attribute.

Operators for Boolean

Only the standard operators (equals, set, not set) are available.

Named Filters

ReqIF Studio provides a mechanism for saving filters, in order
to allow reuse. Filters are saved within the project and can be
applied to ReqIF files within a project.

> Please note that applying filters to other ReqIF files
> within the same project will not work. ReqIF Studio
> will insert an empty filter, which need to be removed or
> reconstructed manually.

By saving the filter for the project as a whole, they will survive
if the file is renamed, as long as it stays in the project.

The filters are managed from the panel shown on the bottom
of the filter panel, as shown in Figure 7.16. To create a named
filter, enter the name in the text box and press SAVE.

Figure 7.16: Controls for managing named filters

The combo dropdown contains all named filters. After selecting them, a number of operations on the chosen filter are possible:

Load. If the name in the combo does exist as a named filter, it can be loaded with LOAD. The current filter settings will be lost.

Save. If the name in the combo does not exist as a named filter yet, SAVE will create a new named filter.

Update. If the name in the combo does exist as a named filter, UPDATE will override it with the current filter configuration.

Delete. If the name in the combo does exist as a named filter, DELETE will remove it. This will not affect the current filter settings.

Filters can be renamed in two steps: By saving an existing filter with a new name, and then deleting the old filter.

7.7.3   Raw ReqIF Search

The raw search feature has been described in the Formal Mind Blog[15].

---

[15]http://formalmind.com/en/blog/formalmind-studio-pror-improvements-and-beta-program-about-start

Bibliography

[Formal Mind, 2016] Formal Mind (since 2016). ReqIF.academy
– an Online-Library for ReqIF and Requirements Exchange.
https://reqif.academy.

[Jastram, 2013] Jastram, M. (2013). The Eclipse Requirements Modeling Framework. In Maalej, W. and
Thurimella, A., editors, *Managing Requirements Knowledge*. Springer. http://www.stups.uni-duesseldorf.de/w/Special:
Publication/RMF_Mark_Book_Jastram_2013.

[Jastram, 2014] Jastram, M. (2014). Open Up - How the ReqIF
Standard for Requirements Exchange Disrupts the Tool Market. *IREB Requirements Engineering Magazine*, 3. http://re-magazine.ireb.org/issues/2014-3-gaining-height/open-up/.

Index

www.ingramcontent.com/pod-product-compliance
Lightning Source LLC
Chambersburg PA
CBHW071222050326
40689CB00011B/2413